John White Chadwick

The Faith of Reason

A Series of Discourses on the leading Topics of Religion

John White Chadwick

The Faith of Reason
A Series of Discourses on the leading Topics of Religion

ISBN/EAN: 9783744745413

Printed in Europe, USA, Canada, Australia, Japan

Cover: Foto ©Lupo / pixelio.de

More available books at **www.hansebooks.com**

THE

FAITH OF REASON.

A Series of Discourses

ON

THE LEADING TOPICS OF RELIGION.

By JOHN W. CHADWICK,
AUTHOR OF "THE BIBLE OF TO-DAY."

BOSTON:
ROBERTS BROTHERS.
1879.

My darling boy, kissed but a moment since,
And laid away all rosy in the dark
Is talking to himself. What does he say?
Not much, in truth, that I can understand;
But now and then, among the pretty sounds
That he is making, falls upon my ear
My name. And then the sand-man softly comes
Upon him and he sleeps.

And what am I,
Here in my book, but as a little child
Trying to cheer the big and silent dark
With foolish words? But listen, O, my God,
My Father, and among them thou shalt hear
Thy name. And soon I too shall sleep.
When I awake I shall be still with thee.

PREFACE.

THIS volume is made up of a series of discourses preached in rapid succession to my own people in the months of January and February, 1879. It may be that some apology is due to the general reader for the directness of their form, and for some passages that make him a party to the confidential talk of a minister to his congregation. But the fact that the volume is printed in accordance with the expressed desire of my habitual hearers, and is intended primarily for their perusal, is my excuse for retaining the original form of its constituent parts. If reason as well as excuse is needed, let it be that the directness of their method is so deeply implicated in the various discourses, that to eliminate it wholly would be to change their character so much that with less trouble I could re-write the entire series. I am persuaded that the form will prove no serious embarrassment to the general reader. Besides I have no desire to make the volume appear other than it is,—a collection of discourses on the leading topics of religion, written with reference to current discussions, and in answer to questions put to me by the more earnest and thoughtful members of my congregation.

BROOKLYN, October 25, 1879.

CONTENTS.

Introductory Discourses.

		PAGE
I.	AGNOSTIC RELIGION	13
II.	THE NATURE OF RELIGION	41

The Faith of Reason.

III.	CONCERNING GOD	72
IV.	CONCERNING IMMORTALITY	113
V.	CONCERNING PRAYER	161
VI.	CONCERNING MORALS	209

INTRODUCTORY DISCOURSES.

I THINK man's soul dwells nearer to the East,
Nearer to morning's fountains than the sun;
Herself the source whence all tradition sprang,
Herself at once both labyrinth and clew.
The miracle fades out of history,
But faith and wonder and the primal earth
Are born into the world with every child.
LOWELL.

THAT one Face does not vanish, rather grows;
Or decomposes but to recompose;
Becomes my Universe that feels and knows.
ROBERT BROWNING.

O POWER, more near my life than life itself,
I fear not thy withdrawal; more I fear,
Seeing, to know thee not, hoodwinked with dreams
Of signs and wonders, while, unnoticed, thou
Walking thy garden still, commun'st with men,
Missed in the commonplace of miracle.
LOWELL.

I.

AGNOSTIC RELIGION.

"ONE can begin so many things with a new person," says George Eliot, "even to be a better man." Why not with a new year as well as with a new person? Somehow the aspect of the season seems to lend itself to thoughts of hope and cheer. The outward aspect of the days is hardly any different from those immediately preceding. The sun rises a few minutes later than it did, and lengthens out each day a little at the end; a lazy way of lengthening his days, at first, as if it came a little hard to him. But the inward aspect somehow is not the same. A week ago, the backward look was natural, but now the forward look is so. Even those of you who have fared the worst of late are beginning to see light ahead. The fresh new year shall see you on your feet again before it die, and marching on to victory.

What I propose to do this morning is to avail myself of this courageous attitude in which you find yourselves, and invite your attention to a subject which would not perhaps have been appropriate to the more sombre mood which was engendered by your old-year meditations. I am aware that such a course is open to the objection that it is a sort of death's-head at the feast; but I remember that the purpose of that same death's-head was not to chill the merriment, but rather to encourage it with a somewhat grim and yet good-natured *carpe diem* — Seize on to-day. What I wish to do is to consider certain tendencies of modern thought; also the goal to which they seem to tend; and then to ask as fearlessly and answer as frankly as possible the question, Supposing that these tendencies go on and ultimate, will there be any thing left to mankind that can properly be called religion; and, if so, will it be any thing that will be worth the sympathy and loyalty of earnest and true-hearted men and women?

The tendencies to which I refer are far less

noticeable here in America than they are in England and upon the Continent. Or perhaps a truer statement would be that here they attain to much less frequent and important literary expression. But, before going further, I am in duty bound to state what tendencies I have in mind. They are not such as have for their objective point the denial of the dogmas of our popular theology, nor even such as contravene its fundamental assumption of the supernatural origin of Christianity. Those tendencies are ubiquitous and positive enough, but their significance is slight in comparison with other tendencies, hardly less ubiquitous and hardly less positive. But these attain to much less frequent and expansive and well-ordered literary expression. They have no respectable organ here in America, so far as I am able to discover. "The Index," which is edited by my noble friend Francis Ellingwood Abbot, is certainly respectable; but it is not the organ of agnosticism, of nescience, much less of dogmatic denial. Mr. Abbot himself is not an atheist, but a rational theist, able he thinks to give a reason for the faith that is in him. Nevertheless, the tendencies which I have in mind find more conspicuous expression in his paper than in any other of equal intellectual force and general refinement.

These tendencies, as I have now sufficiently implied, are those whose ultimate goal is the denial of any positive reality corresponding to the terms, God, Immortality, Prayer. Of private expression of these tendencies here in America, there is certainly no lack. And, judging from my personal experience, for every person affected by these tendencies a dozen years ago, there are a score affected by them now. Notably scientific men, albeit professors in the most orthodox colleges, and regular attendants upon such "means of grace" as are provided by the college authorities for the benefit of the rising generation, confess to you when they are off duty that, corresponding to the words which I have named above, they are aware of no substantial meanings. Even the late Professor Agassiz, who, in default of better, publicly attacked Darwin with the *ad captandum* argument, "We are not the children of monkeys: we are the children of God," said to me privately in just so many words, "Mr. Chadwick, the scientific man knows nothing about God." But the tendencies which I have named are not confined to scientific men. I find them everywhere where there are thoughtful men and women; not such as are hilariously happy in their discovery that there is no God, no immortality, and that every spoken prayer is so much wasted breath, though many such there are; but there are also those to whom the loss of these convictions and ideas out of their anxious lives is an immeasurable sorrow, who yet, because they cannot or think they cannot honestly retain them, with moistened eye and trembling lip bid them a sad farewell. There is one man here in America, who, better perhaps than any other, publicly represents the tendencies I have in mind; in whom indeed, if I am not mistaken, they have reached their ultimate goal of absolute nescience. I refer to Mr. Felix Adler. Refined, scholarly, reverent, intensely moral, ardently benevolent, with a genuine enthusiasm for humanity, he does not say, There is no God, There is no immortality, but he does say, If there be a God or immortality, we have no knowledge of the one or of the other, and he says that prayer is a survival of beliefs which we no longer entertain, with which it ought to be discarded.

In some respects, England is a much freer country than the United States. The tyranny of public opinion is much more repressive here than there. It is quite possible that there is much less of Mr. Adler's style of thought here than in England. But what there is, is much more timid in its expression here than there. There, there is so much of it, and it has grown so much of late, that they have made a new word to express it, — *agnosticism* (*a* is the negative, and *gnosticism* means knowing or knowledge; and so *agnosticism* is literally *not knowing*, and an *agnostic* is *one who does not know*). The creation of these words, and the frequent use of them of late, — you must all of you have come upon them many times, —

are signs of the increasing prevalence of the things which they denote. The increasing use of the word *nescience*, the negative opposite of science in its primitive sense, knowledge, is another finger pointing in the same direction. Those of our periodicals which reprint the most striking English articles introduce to the American public many of the agnostic articles that appear in England, but only a small proportion of them all. To one who follows up the course of English thought in the reviews and magazines pretty closely, nothing is more impressive than the extent to which the agnostic element prevails in such literature, as well as in scores of books, and the rapidity with which it has increased within a dozen years. The "Fortnightly Review" is virtually the organ of agnostic thought, and its editor, John Morley, is a man whose culture and ability are second to no man's in Great Britain. But his review does not monopolize all the agnosticism. It appears in the "Contemporary" and the "Nineteenth Century," side by side with the pretentious vaporings of cardinals and bishops. It appears almost everywhere. Men of the highest social, scientific, and literary rank make no concealment of their utter lack of faith in any God or immortality. And what is so obvious in Great Britain will shortly be so in America. If you and I were cowards, we should try perhaps to blink these facts, to make believe that no such facts exist. But they would exist just the same for all our cowardliness and lying. However it may be with others, whatever faith *I* have must be in spite of all that I can hear or read against it. If I should catch myself wilfully trying to believe one thing or another, not seeking for the truth, but seeking for arguments to bolster up some preconceived opinion, I should be ashamed ever to face you in this place again. Very likely, if I had avoided all the way along every book of less conservative aspect than my own thought, I might have remained just where I was a dozen years ago, or even have gone the way of various others, back to the flesh-pots of the popular theology. And it may be that I have read too exclusively the most iconoclastic writers who have challenged my beliefs. If it has been so, you may at least congratulate yourselves that the opinions which I have presented to you have not been drifted to my feet by any tide of mere conventionality, but have been plucked out of the teeth of danger, and fought for upon many a painfully contested field.

From twelve to twenty years ago, when the supernatural theory of Christianity, the special inspiration of the Bible, and so on, were being summoned sharply to the bar of reason, there were those who said that the process of negation would not end with any of these things. It would go on, they said, till it involved the faiths of natural religion in a common ruin with supernatural Christianity. But those who said these things were, like Cassandra, doomed to have their prophecies habitually disbelieved and disregarded. I know that I for one did not believe them or regard them. The supernatural, I thought, was but a parasitic growth, which had sucked, was sucking, and would suck, the life out of natural religion. Destroy this parasitic growth, thought I,— and I was one of many who thought so,— and natural religion would at once renew its youth, bourgeon and blossom out as it had never done before, and bear such fruit of joy and blessing as had never gladdened the eyes and fed the hungry hearts of men since time began. But the Cassandras were right. Supernatural religion has everywhere lost its hold on the intelligence of the civilized world, and so has natural religion, too, in any such concrete shape as men imagined its triumphant future. If Theodore Parker, for example, could come back to us, he would confess that things had taken quite a different turn from that which he anticipated and predicted. He would find a thousand ready to accept his anti-supernaturalism where he found a score when he was in the flesh. But would he find them all as confident as he was of a perfect God, a glorious immortality; all of them ready to sanction his old-time prayers, wherein he talked with God as naturally and simply as a boy with his own mother? No, he would not. He would find in many instances that these things which were more dear to him than his own life had gone the way of others which were to him hateful and intolerable to the last degree. I am sure that Mr. Froude does not exaggerate when he says that there is silently transpiring in our midst a more important change in thought than any which the world has undergone since the downfall of Paganism and the conversion of the Roman Empire. I doubt if he would have exaggerated if he had said that even this was less important than the change which is at present going on.

Now it is no part of my scheme this morning to state the arguments for or against one or the other of those great doctrines which have heretofore been deemed essential to religion. I will only say that, because the tendency of late has been so strong either to dogmatic denial of these doctrines or to agnostic inability to assent to them, it does not follow that this tendency is absolutely just, and that we should all at once and all together abandon ourselves to it without reserve, as if its ultimate must be the final good. The tendency of thought at any given time may be in quite the opposite direction from that "final philosophy" which a Princeton Professor imagines he has discovered and condensed into one bulky volume, but which is still, I fancy, far, far ahead of us. There are those who speak as if the tendency of thought at any given time being discovered, there was nothing else for us to do, but drop our oars and let it bear us as it will upon its bosom. But sometimes there is nothing else for us to do, so we be men not things, than to contend against it with all our strength. And there is sometimes nothing else than this for us to do when the tendency of thought for the time being is towards the perfect. If it does not seem so to us, then we must go the other way. The band of Arctic explorers who patiently and painfully walked towards the North day after day, and then discovered they had been walking on an immense ice-floe all the time, which had taken them hundreds of miles southward, nevertheless did well to do just as they did. They knew the way their feet were going; they did not know there was a mighty current sweeping them at its own will. And so it often is with us. The mighty sweep of things, the ultimate tendency which gathers up into itself all aberrations and divergences,—just as a ship's course to her destination all of her tackings on and off,— of this we cannot be aware. We are on an ice-floe of such vast extent that, with strained eye or telescope, we have never seen its utmost bound. What we *can* know is whether our own feet are keeping on, however wearily and painfully, towards that which seems to us to be the true and good. If they are doing this, then we may look the whole world in the face without one blush of shame. It is here, I think, that rationalists are often quite as narrow, quite as unjust, as the most bigoted supernaturalists. They blame this or that person for not going with them, when he does not go with them simply and only because they do not seem to him to be going towards the truth. Instead of blaming him for his refusal to accept their guidance, they should admire him for his steadfastness to personal convictions, — a nobler thing in any man than following, if this were possible, the absolute truth without such steadfastness.

On the other hand, it is no less certain that if the facts which come within our ken seem hostile to those doctrines and ideas which we regard as most essential to religion, seem wholly subversive of them, then there is nothing else for us to do but to accept this conclusion manfully and adjust our lives to it as best we can. Whatever is doubtful, one thing is certain, — that no real good can come to us except along the line of our own personal integrity of thought and deed. It may well be that the negations of the present time are but so many steps in a progress to some higher affirmation than the world has ever yet received. I believe this. In hours of higher sanity, of deeper thought, I seem to catch some glimpses of a far-off time when man shall have a thought of God, of immortality, of prayer, more grand and beautiful than any thought of these which has so far appealed to the intelligence of men. But, however this may be, nothing remains for us but to accept that which we are convinced is true, to give up every thing which does not seem so any longer. It may be hard, but if it is our duty, then there is no more to say. And, however some of us may conscientiously abide in a more positive order of ideas, let us beware lest we should ever cast the faintest shadow of reproach on those who have been inwardly compelled to surrender every most distinctive article of natural religion as it has so far been conceived. If they are as narrow and bitter in their iconoclasm as others are in their conservatism, then we may blame their narrowness and bigotry. But you and I have many a friend whose agnosticism is complete, but whose fidelity to personal conviction puts to shame our own and that of our most orthodox acquaintances. For such we have no words of blame, and even our pity seems to find no joint in their self-poise and self-respect which it can penetrate.

The aim of my discourse is not to question the validity of any of the leading doctrines of religion, or to analyze the processes by which these doctrines have lost their hold upon so many minds, but simply, facing, for the time, the fact that there are many minds on which their hold is broken, to ask, What then? Does any thing remain to such that can with any justness or propriety be spoken of as religion; and, if so, what is the nature and the good of it?

I find the question stated in a recent number of the " London Spectator " in a bit of verse: —

> " What is the good and what is the bad?
>   What is the perfectly true?
> What is the end you live for, my lad,
>   And what may I ask are you?
> Unproven I fear is your heaven above;
>   Life is but labor and sorrow;
> Then why should we hope, and why should we love,
>   And why should we care for the morrow?"

And not only is the question put, but also the following answer: —

> "There may be a fight worth fighting, my friend,
>   Though victory there be none;
> And though no haven be ours at the end,
>   Still we may steer straight on.
> And though nothing be good and nothing be bad
>   And nothing be true to the letter,
> Yet a good many things are worse, my lad,
>   And one or two things are better."

The scope of this question and answer is indeed somewhat wider than that of my own question as I have stated it above. These introduce the ethical problem from which so far I have kept myself clear. The average assumption of the agnostic thinker is that, when we come to ethics, we come to *terra firma*. But recently various writers have been arguing, very laboriously, to prove that morals are dependent on religion, and that with the dogmatic denial of God and immortality, or the agnostic refusal to make either of these affirmations, the ground of all morality is cut away under its feet. Into the merits of this controversy, I have been with you already. Suffice it now to say that we arrived at the conclusion that, whatever inspiration or incitement for ethical action resides in the convictions corresponding to the terms God and Immortality, the basis of morals is in the social life of man, — in the absolute necessity for men who are to live together in harmonious relations to accept certain limits to their conduct, to forego certain acts, however pleasant, because they are anti-social in their nature, and to perform certain others, however painful, because the social good demands them. The importance of moral actions does not lie in their determination of the happiness or misery of individual men beyond the grave, but in their determination of the happiness or misery of the agent and of society here in this present world. Instead of saying, therefore, "Let us eat and drink, for to-morrow we die," if we have no longer any faith in an immortal life beyond the grave, we should say, Let us eat and drink, temperately and wisely, for to-day we live, and shall live well or ill in part according as we manage well or ill this bodily structure which is so closely implicated with the fortunes of our intellect and will. And as morality is not dependent on any theory of a future life, so is it not dependent upon any theory of God. That it is not dependent upon God, I do by no means say. For to my mind, in the last analysis, he is "the power not ourselves that makes for righteousness." But whether a man conceives him so or not, he cannot but admit that there is such a power, and he may still be moral, intensely so, whatever theory he may have of it. Ay, though, with or without the adjunct of a God, a man should hold with Schopenhauer and Hartmann that this is the worst possible world, I do not see that the foundations of morality would even then be shaken. On the contrary, I have often wondered if pessimism be not a better working creed than optimism. If this is the best possible world, as Leibnitz taught, to endeavor to improve it would appear to be an idle task. But if this is the worst possible world, it still remains for us to better it a little if we can. So much then, at least, remains for the agnostic, — "mere morality." Of God and immortality he may not presume to speak, and prayer may seem to him an idle form of words. But duty still remains. He is still living in a social world where his own actions do not end in themselves, but affect the welfare of others in ever-widening circles and to the remotest generations. The experience of innumerable generations has wrought out for him a moral code, which, although still capable of further emendation, is not to be lightly set aside. So much remains to the agnostic thinker. All arguments to the contrary are so many brilliant *tours de force* by which it is attempted to terrify men back into the beliefs they have discarded, — a process morally akin to threats of pincers, rack, and wheel. Let the *a priori* reasoner prove ever so conclusively that the unbelieving man cannot be moral, and lo, his next-door neighbor is an unbeliever, the whiteness of whose moral nature, the courage of whose moral action, puts his own to shame. Ah! but, says Mr. Mallock, his morality is only a survival of the beliefs his ancestors once held. It is a convenient subterfuge. An unbelieving community, we are assured, or one which had worked out the entire stock of its hereditary faith, would not be moral. Such a contingency is so remote that it is very safe to prophesy. Meantime what we are certain of is, that men whose faith is of the smallest in those doctrines of religion which are considered most essential are moral peers of the most enthusiastic believers of their own or any other time. Of this we are entirely certain; about the other it remains to be seen.

But there are those who think that, properly speaking, morality is no part of religion. For better or for worse, the two have been associated from the earliest times; but if nothing more remains to the agnostic, they would say, than "mere morality," albeit there is nothing else in the whole world so good as this, they do not think he can be justly said to have any thing which is really of the nature of religion. Does there, then, remain to the agnostic any thing but mere morality, any thing which has either the form or essence of religion over and above its moral elements? There certainly does, if those who accept Comte in his entirety have any right to answer. These, answering for themselves, insist that they have a religion which is just as truly a religion as the Romanist's or Calvinist's. It has no God; it has no immortality; though it has a kind of prayer.

But it has a substitute for God, namely, *Le Grand Etre*, the Great Being, Humanity, past, present, and future. It has a substitute for immortality, — the perpetuity of social influence; and that it is no ignoble one let George Eliot's poem testify, the grandest poem of these latter days: —

"Oh, may I join the choir invisible!"

It has a substitute for prayer, — ascriptions of reverence and adoration to the spirits of great men and saintly women who have been incorporated into the Great Being. And yet, although the religion of humanity, as this is called, is capable of very grand expression, and though it corresponds to a circle of ideas which is full of goodly inspiration, is it not, after all, a sort of make-believe religion? Its god, its immortality, its prayer, are *substitutes* for the God and immortality and prayer of *bonâ fide* religion, and excellent as substitutes; and if my question were, What substitutes are there for God and immortality with the agnostic who has completely lost his faith in these? I might assign to them a very honorable place.

Setting aside, then, the so-called religion of humanity, does there remain to the agnostic any thing of the essence of religion after he feels himself compelled to say, "If there is any God, I cannot find him; if there is any immortality, I cannot prove it: and that God interferes to answer any human prayer I cannot find a particle of warrant." I do not think that I am anxious to make out a case in the affirmative, but only to find out the truth; but I will not deny that I am very happy when the truth appears to be that the most vital essence of religion may remain to one who finds himself compelled to make the above disclaimers. For the most vital essence of religion is not involved in any theory of God or of the world, nor in any theory of human destiny, nor in any form of prayer which needs an interfering deity. The most vital essence of religion is not involved in any of these distinctions of personal and impersonal. Least of all are those to be accounted atheists who cannot speak of God as personal. Spinoza could not so speak of him, and yet Novalis rightly said of him, "He was a God-intoxicated man," and Schleiermacher, "Spinoza not believe in God! My friends, he did not believe in any thing else." Mind you that here I am not pleading for myself; for, if I cared to be dogmatic about the mysteries of the Godhead, I should say, To predicate personality of the Infinite is to express the inexpressible a little better than to predicate impersonality. But may we not go one step further, and declare that the most vital essence of religion is not involved in any theory of God whatever, or even in any affirmation of a being who is the moving force of all phenomena? To affirm God is to affirm a theory of the universe; to me a theory of all-sufficing excellence and absolutely indispensable. I can conceive that all the harmonious order of the universe was potential in that vaporous cloud which was the primordial substance of the world, but only if there was potential in it antecedent to the lowest term of the ascending series, a higher than the highest. Evolution of a higher *from* a lower is comprehensible enough. But evolution of a higher *by* a lower is absolutely incomprehensible. To affirm God, then, is to affirm a theory of the universe; most indispensable, but still a theory. And the most vital essence of religion is not involved in man's relation to any theory of the universe, but in his relation to the universe itself. It is to be impressed with its majestic order, to thrill with recognition of the tender grace and awful sweep of things, and to convert this passive recognition into a voluntary energy of devotion to the eternal order in which we find ourselves embosomed. And even for the complete agnostic there may remain this vital essence of religion. He may discard all theories, but he cannot discard the universe. Evermore his little life is set in the midst of this abounding order, mystery, and law. And the question, Is he a religious man? is answered, not by discovering what theory he has of God or of the universe, but by discovering in what attitude he stands before the everlasting fact. If in an attitude of easy indifference or unawed garrulity, then truly he is not a religious man. But if the morning and the evening hush, the glow at night of multitudinous stars, the "spring's delicious trouble in the ground," the summer's beautiful effulgence, the imperial splendor of autumnal days, and, more than all, the mystery of human life and thought and love, — if all these things gladden his heart so much that he cannot express his joy, and yet soften it so that suddenly it overflows with unforbidden tears, then he may well be more religious than one who has a theory of God or of the universe which he can rattle off to you as glibly as a boy his morning lesson. And though such a man may never pray in any form of words, and least of all may ever wish to coax the Infinite to interfere to turn his mill or sell his merchandise, or even to make him a better man, which he can do at any time himself by simply availing himself of the normal structure of the universe,—nevertheless when this man looks up to heaven at night, or out upon the sea, or into faces that respond to him with eye-beams full of love, or into the immeasurable deeps of his own moral nature, the awe that falls upon his heart, the joy with which it leaps, the peace that passes understanding and subdues him utterly, is just as truly prayer as any form of words that ever trembled with the fervor of a saint's most passionate entreaty.

You may think, perhaps, that I have been a long way round, and taken a great deal of trouble to show that men and women who declare that they have no religion may nevertheless have a religion of the most genuine sort. You may think they will not thank me for my trouble. Well, what I have written has not been written with a view to getting their thanks. It has been written to express my gratitude and joy that religion, equally with morality, is so independent of all special theories, so deeply implicated in the total make of things, that where there is intelligence and earnestness there must be religion. Hundreds are busy in our time in trying to convince their neighbors that unless they believe thus and so they are religious or moral under false pretences; that unless they believe thus and so they have no right to be moral or religious. But mine has been a far more gracious task: to show that morals have their basis in no theological conceptions, but in the natural relationships of human life; to show that even religion in its divinest essence is not man's sense of his relation to any theory of the universe, however pure and high, but is rather his sense, tender and awful, sweet and strong and sane, of his relation to the universe itself. I do not know what better New-Year's greeting I could give you than this assurance, that wherever there is intelligence and earnestness, there religion is as inevitable as to a living man the beating of his heart. Religion may be vastly more than this inevitable relation between the finite and the infinite, but this must ever be the brightest jewel in its crown.

JANUARY 5, 1879.

II.

THE NATURE OF RELIGION.

LAST Sunday morning, it was my happy privilege to invite you, each and all, to come and rejoice with me that religion is so deeply implicated in the make of things, the structure of mankind, that where there is earnestness and intelligence there must be religion. The most of you accepted my invitation joyfully. From time to time, you had been troubled by your apparent obligation to deny the possession of religion to certain of your friends and neighbors, whose apparent irreligiousness, or, rather, unreligion, seemed to suggest a doubt whether religion after all is of any great importance. If some of the best men you know have no religion, religion cannot, it would seem, be quite that indispensable thing which we have heretofore imagined it to be. All those among you who have had some such experience as this were very glad, I think, that, without any forcing of the facts, I could so easily make it appear that the essential virtue of religion is not involved in any theory or definition, but in man's attitude of reverence and loyalty before this Everlasting Fact we call the Universe. Others among you were, perhaps, somewhat differently affected. Certain religious beliefs are to you so important, that you have come to regard them as absolutely essential to religion; to feel that a man is religious under false pretences, that a man has no right to be religious, who does not very consciously and definitely believe in God and Immortality and Prayer. And some of you were so unfortunate as to identify my own position with that of the persons I was speaking of, though I took particular pains to avoid any such misunderstanding. I sometimes think that preachers are the victims of a horrible fatality, in virtue of which their hearers are seized with a sudden anxiety about the temperature of the church, or whether somebody else will not object to what the preacher is saying, just at the moment when he is saying something which he is particularly anxious they should hear. And so it happens, when he has dipped his pen in the ink thirty or forty times without writing a word, debating with himself whether he shall call a thing invisible blue or invisible green, they go away with the idea that he said it was as black as a coal, or holding him responsible for an opinion which he has stated only with a view to expressing his partial or entire dissent.

The leading thought of my discourse[1] last Sunday morning was one which has long been exceedingly precious and consoling to my mind, but it was not one in which I have any special and exclusive property. It has been carefully elaborated and eloquently enforced by J. Allanson Picton, an English Trinitarian clergyman, whose book, "The Mystery of Matter," is the most helpful and instructive volume I have read for the last dozen years. But it was not original with him. "The Nation," of some recent date, speaking of the poet Shelley, says that he " re-

[1] On "Agnostic Religion," p. 13.

jected all that is properly known as Christianity, and that it is impossible to deny his atheism;" and yet, "in all that constituted a religious mind, in natural piety, in purity of life and motive, Shelley was exceptionally conspicuous." But of this seeming paradox "The Nation" finds abundant confirmation in the statement of the late Frederick Robertson, that "with all his scepticism, Shelley's disposition was any thing but irreligious." "A person of much eminence for piety in our times," says Robertson, "has well observed that the greatest want of religious feeling is not to be found among the greatest infidels, but among those who never think of religion except as a matter of course." "The leading feature of Shelley's character," he continues, "may be said to have been a natural piety." It is not uncommon for Christian people to allow that such or such a person, however sceptical, is "a good man;" but you will notice that what Robertson claims for Shelley, who was no mere agnostic, but a dogmatic atheist, if there ever was one, is "a natural piety," — a sentiment which preachers who have not a thousandth part of Robertson's spirituality, are apt to think impossible save in connection with a very definite idea of God, and a very frank and positive belief in him. You will see, then, that for the doctrine of my discourse I did not lack the enthusiastic support of two at least (Picton and Robertson) of the most gifted evangelical Christians of these modern times. Without their support, I should feel equally certain, not only of the truth, but of the joy and satisfaction inherent in my view; but if any of you sigh to have the truth I hold indorsed by orthodox authorities, you are entirely welcome to the facts as I have stated them.

After so much of a prelude to my discourse, let me proceed at once to the discussion of the question, *What is religion?* — a question which I wish to answer in a general way before taking up some of the leading doctrines of religion, and making them the subjects of a series of discourses. My purpose is not now, as last Sunday morning, to discover the most vital essence of religion, but to discover, first, its relative significance, then the course of its development, and, finally, the highest form it can assume consistently with the idea which I have already set forth of its most vital essence.

What is religion? It is the most significant factor in the history of mankind. I know that there are those who think, or think they think, that religion is a matter of the past; that it has seen its best days, and is now seeing its worst, — the days of its humiliation and decay; unless they should prefer to call the days of its power and triumph its worst days, — worst for mankind, — and these its best, because well-nigh its last. But even they would not be able to deny that in the past the religious life has been the most conspicuous and important interest. Religion has been the most engrossing theme of the historian; it has built the grandest buildings, written the most precious books, painted the most beautiful pictures, suggested the most glorious music, inspired the most illustrious men, inaugurated the most important changes of society, controlled the most far-reaching movements of mankind. Religion was the fountain-head of all the ancient arts. Literature was invented to immortalize her ethics and her prayers; astronomy, to ferret out the secrets of her starry gods; sculpture, to make visible her deities; architecture, to enshrine the sculptor's work; mathematics, to mark out her festivals, the song and dance to gladden them. It is a notable fact that even those who are at present most convinced that religion has had its day, do not find any other problems so fascinating and engrossing as those furnished by her vicissitudes. Dead she may be, yet they are never tired of groping in her tomb, of studying out the footprints she has made across the centuries. Even her childhood, feeble and stammering, as all childhood is, has kept hundreds of scholars busy day and night during the present century, until at length, in his "Principles of Sociology," the indefatigable and faithful Spencer has been able to gather up into a graphic and consistent whole the story of her birth and infant ways, — so charming some of them in their absurdity, — in a way that leaves almost nothing for his successors to do but to add comment and illustration to his comprehensive and convincing argument. In all of this, I am aware there is no argument for the continuance of any special form of religion. But there is an argument for the belief that there must be something essential to humanity in that which has been so vast, so multiform, so universal, so far-dating in its manifestations. Modern opponents of religion are, for the most part, great believers in the power and dignity of human nature. But could human nature be convicted of hopeless idiocy in any other way more forcibly than by the assurance that all its interest in religion, from first to last, has been a grand mistake? Banish the religions, each and all, but only that *religion* may the more remain! That which has been so long in coming to maturity will never perish in a night. The mushroom may do that, but not the oak, whose roots have sucked its life-blood from the soil, whose strength has matched itself against a century of storms.

At the same time, it would be almost criminal for us to overlook the fact that such a vast amount of evil has been associated with religion in the past, that it is no wonder that many have sincerely doubted whether the good associated with it has been of equal weight.

"We cannot forget," says Dr. Hedge, "that religion has been a worker of evil, — one of the greatest of the workers of evil. No agent that has wrought in earthly scenes has been more prolific of ruin and wrong. The wildest aberrations of human nature, crimes the most portentous, the most desolating wars, persecutions, hatred and wrath and bloodshed, more than have flowed from all sources beside, — have been its fruits. The victims of fanaticism outnumber those of every other and all other passions that have wasted the earth. Pining in dungeons, hunted like beasts of prey, stretched on the rack, affixed to the cross, — their sufferings are the horror of history. No high-wrought fiction, recounting imaginary woes, can match the colors of their authentic tragedy. A corrup-

"tion of the text of the Vedas has cast thousands
"of Hindu widows alive on the funeral-pile. An
"interpolation of two words in the service of the
"Eastern Church has driven whole villages in
"Russia into fiery death. A sentence in the
"Book of Exodus has been a death-sentence to
"millions of hapless women. And who shall
"compute the sum of the lives that have fur-
"nished the holocausts of the Inquisition?

'Tantum religio potuit suadere malorum.'

"In this tale of sorrows we must reckon, more-
"over, the melancholy and madness religion so
"often engenders, — religious mania,— which,
"where it does not impel to self-slaughter, op-
"presses the soul with dull despair, or pierces
"it with mortal anguish. It is fearful to think
"that man, in addition to the necessary bur-
"dens of life and all inevitable ills, should
"be subject to these ideal woes; that so many
"fine spirits should suffer blight through their
"own diseased imaginations; that to so many
"noble minds the light that is in them should be

"made darkness through superstitious doubts and fears; that so many innocent hearts should bear the burden of self-imputed guilt and doom! No region of the earth, and no plane of life, is secure from this plague. Bayard Taylor found in the track of the missionaries beyond the Arctic circle the same spiritual ails that have desolated polished lands. 'The soul,' says Novalis, 'is the most active of poisons.' Religion is the soul of mortal life; when mis-directed or over-urged it becomes, instead of an animating force, a consuming fire."

This is, indeed, a serious indictment of religion, but, coming as it does from one of its most thoughtful advocates, it cannot be suspected of over-statement. But there has been a great waste of abuse of religion on account of this dark side of its development, which hundreds of would-be evolutionists still keep up, though in strict accordance with the terms of their philosophy, they have no right to do so. All such abuse presupposes the supernatural standpoint. Your ardent evolutionist, in nine cases out of ten, speaks of religion as if it had been made complete outside of human nature, and imposed upon it, when, in fact, human nature itself has made it, and it has been good or bad just in proportion as human nature has been the one or the other. "Imposed by priests?" Ay, but the priests are self-imposed, legitimate children of humanity. Religion has kept pace with human culture. At every stage, it has been the best religion possible. Nothing, seen from our standpoint, can be more puerile than the earliest ideas of religion; but, with the data which men had at their command, they were the most reasonable possible, and did as much credit to their inventors as the ideas of Martineau and Tyndall and Spencer do to them. It is high time for men to stop blaming religion for her debasing treatment of humanity, seeing that she is humanity's own child, and ever bears her parent's image in her face.

What is religion? It is an order of ideas and beliefs and practices which includes, upon the one hand, the humblest worship of ancestral ghosts, — a stage antecedent to fetichism, — and on the other hand, the silence of a Carlyle or Spencer before the Infinities and Immensities, and all that lies between this zenith and that nadir. And nowhere, along the course of this development, is there a break at which a supernatural element can be intruded, while the wild growth of supernatural theories can easily be accounted for without recourse to any supernatural facts. Religion is often spoken of as if it were cöextensive with humanity. But investigation seems to show that there are tribes still extant which have stopped short of religion in their development. Antecedent to religion there must be a regular development of ideas concerning sleep and dreams and swoon and epilepsy, of death and resurrection, of souls and ghosts, spirits, and demons. Religion does not properly begin before the supernatural agent has, as it were, forgotten his human origin, or at least ceased to be regarded as the special ancestor or friend. The realm of ghosts develops into a realm of supernatural agents, who have lost their ancestral traits and special relationships, before religion can properly be said to have begun. Whether or not, then, "*we* are such stuff as dreams are made of," our religion is, most clearly, in the last analysis. It was the hush of consciousness in sleep that suggested to primeval men an inner-self who could go wandering off, leaving the body dull and silent, and come back to revive it. The analogy of sleep and death was too conspicuous to admit a moment's doubt that death was but a sleep, during which the other self might, *must* still be alive and stirring. It is hardly to be wondered at that ideas of a future life have engrossed so much attention in the religious sphere when we consider that the genesis of these ideas was actually antecedent to the genesis of religion. The ghosts were the progenitors of the gods. There was a doctrine of immortality before there was a doctrine of religion. And it may well be, also, that the moral idea was other-worldly in its earliest form; that the rights of ghostly ancestors took chronological as well as logical precedence of the rights of living men and women. Given the conviction of a world of ghosts, and every subsequent step in the development from ancestor-worship to fetichism, from fetichism to nature-worship, from nature-worship to polytheism, from polytheism to monotheism, from monotheism as anthropomorphic as possible, — that is, representing the god as much like a man as possible, — to monotheism as little anthropomorphic as possible, — given the starting-point, and every subsequent stage of this process of evolution is inevitable. Strangely enough, — but in the strangeness is there not a hint that the evolution of religion has at length come full circle? — strangely enough, religion ends where it began, — with the affirmation, God is a Spirit. But did ever formal likeness include such utterly divergent thought? The "spirit" of the primeval worshipper was an ancestral *ghost*. And there were as many gods as there were ghosts. For us there is *One God*. *A* spirit? Say rather, dropping the article, who is *spirit*, one, and yet far more omnipresent than all the multitudes of the primeval worshipper.

> "A presence far more deeply interfused,
> Whose dwelling is the light of setting suns,
> And the round ocean and the living air,
> And the blue sky, and in the mind of man, —
> A motion and a spirit that impels
> All thinking things, all objects of all thought,
> And rolls through all things."

There are those who seem to think religion wholly discredited, through all its course, by such an account of its genesis as this which I have given. It began in dreams, they say, and it is still a dream. The last spirit like the first is a film of the imagination. But no beginning, however small and weak, can utterly discredit the consummate fruit of any process of evolution if it so be that the consummate fruit is fair and sweet. Because all apples are descended from the common crab, shall I despise my golden sweets upon yon "holy hill," and shall the Baldwins only blush for shame, and not, as maidens do, for greater loveliness? Is the great ocean steamer any less wonderful and beautiful because her first progenitor was not even a "dug-out," but a charred log in which some savage made his first brief voyage? Does it detract any thing from Brunelleschi's dome, or Milan's miracle of countless spires, that the first essay in architecture was probably the tying together of the top-branches of several trees with some stout twig or vine? Are certain special architectural forms any less beautiful, because in their inception they symbolized men's wonder at the mystery of reproduction? Could they have symbolized any thing more mysterious, any thing more wonderful? And does "the marriage of true minds" admit of any impediment or get any shadow of dishonor on account of any thing that Lubbock and McLennan have written about wife-seizure as the universal form of primitive marriage? The evolutionist is a traitor to his own philosophy when, from the humble origin of any order of ideas, he infers their present worthlessness or any thing to their discredit. For it is essential to the theory of evolution to maintain that every order of ideas is suitable to the time of its appearance and to the grade of mind that gives it birth. But the genesis of religion was not unworthy or ignoble. Primitive religion was the expression of man's awe and wonder in the presence of his own mysterious life. Its genesis, therefore, was not material but spiritual. Thus, in its dawning hour, there was a hint of its noontide magnificence.

So much for the relative importance of religion, and so much for the order of its development. It now remains to ask, What is religion in this fourth quarter of the nineteenth century? Evidently it is no one thing, or if one thing, then *e pluribus unum*; one made up of many. It is an order of ideas and beliefs and practices almost or quite as comprehensive as the entire process of religious evolution from the remotest down to the present time. There is hardly any stage of religious evolution in the past which is not represented by the different religions of to-day which make up the sum of universal religion. And, indeed, just as the present earth is the best book in which to study the geological history of the planet; just as its processes, at present going on, tell pretty much the whole story, explain almost every thing that ever has taken place,—so the present phenomena of religion, the processes at present going on in the religious world, admit us into almost every secret of the ancient world of thought and aspiration. As a high mountain in the tropics reproduces every zone with its appropriate vegetation, so present religion reproduces every zone of man's religious evolution with its appropriate ideas. Around the base, the savage growths of fetichism, and still lower forms, flourish with tropical luxuriance; higher up, the more temperate forms of polytheism and a monotheism still anthropomorphic; and, higher still, the Edelweiss's *noble purity;* nay, but my figure fails me utterly; the mountain's top blossoms as never did the vales below, and heaven is more near, although its stars into more awful spaces seem withdrawn.

The sympathy of religions ought to follow from the apprehension of their natural development, all from the same far-off and poor beginnings. No *one* can toss its head, elate with the assurance of a supernatural origin, quite different from that of all the rest. No one, not even the highest, can look contemptuously on the lowest in the scale; for in that lowest, as in a mirror, it can see the image of its own rude beginning. As the old gravestones used to phrase it: —

"As you are now, so once was I."

But from an order so inclusive, how select the only true religion? Included in this order is the lowest fetichism on the one hand, and on the other the most spiritual ideas. What if we say there is no absolute best; the religion must be proportioned to the general character and culture? The converted cannibal eats his superfluous wife, because she is an obstacle to his Christian baptism. It is not as if we were all obliged to turn eclectics and go about searching for the best religion. What is best for one man is not best for another. Sitting Bull's own religion is probably better for him than James Martineau's would be. As for the higher thought, as Jesus said, "He that is able to receive it, let him receive it." Those that have it need not fear to publish it lest all these Romanists and Evangelical Protestants should suddenly accept it, and find it incompatible with their general character. They will not accept it. What they want is something concrete, tangible. Only with the general enlargement of their minds do men get rid of small ideas. Till then, the new beliefs are mere receptacles which hold the substance of the former creeds and dogmas.

What is best for one man is not best for another. What is best for you and me is that which we now have, amended by the clearer vision of each succeeding day. Whatever joy and blessing of the religious life may be in store for us, one thing is sure, our way to it must be along the path of our own personal conviction.

"The hell from which a lie will keep a man," says George Macdonald, "is doubtless the best place that he can go to;" and may we not add that the god for whose glory we must shun the guidance of the truth is, by this sign, a god whose glory ought to be with us a matter of supreme indifference?

What a great many persons seem to want is some excuse for keeping up the old names, no matter how little of the old meaning is kept along with them. Mr. Joseph Cook's theology is so different from Calvin's, that Calvin would have roasted him with less compunction than Servetus; but modern orthodoxy cannot sufficiently applaud him, because he gives it a lot of lame excuses for still keeping up a show of belief in the old doctrine, though perfectly aware that his trinity is not the old trinity, nor his atonement the old atonement, nor his depravity the old depravity, and so on through all the creeds and articles. And so, I grieve to say, there is some disposition here and there among radical thinkers, who honestly believe that religion is a thing of the past, to make-believe that this or that thing is religion which in reality they do not consider to be so. Here it is the worship of collective humanity, and there the worship of the moral ideal. Again, knowing what prestige the name of religion carries, some endeavor to make out that morality is identical with religion, and co-extensive; while, on the other hand, there are not a few in the community who contend that religion is entirely independent of morality, and that, while morality is an ever-greatening reality, religion is a survival of the past. To neither of these positions can we commit ourselves after a careful study of the facts. To identify morality with religion, to declare that beyond morality religion has no significance, is to go counter to the entire history of religion since it has been historical, and to all the archæologists have raked together beyond the utmost bound of history. The association of morality with religion has always been so close — or if not always, generally — that to call morality an essential part of religion is certainly legitimate. Last Sunday morning I assumed for the moment the negation of this position in order to ask, "If morality is not essential to religion, does any thing remain to the agnostic thinker that can properly be called religion?" But the next moment, spite of myself, I brought it back again, when I said that the most vital essence of religion was to be impressed with the majestic order of the universe, to thrill with recognition of the tender grace and awful sweep of things, and (here the morality came back) *to convert this passive recognition into a voluntary energy of devotion to the eternal order in which we find ourselves embosomed.* And if morality is a part of religion, it must be a great part; if conduct be indeed, as Matthew Arnold has insisted, three-fourths of human life. He has not, I fancy, overrated its importance. But so long as morality responds to purely social inspirations, so long as duty is simply and only a man's contribution to the social order, a man's expression of his gratitude for the fidelity of former generations, it may be said that it is not consciously religious. It is unconsciously religious, because "the power, not ourselves, that makes for righteousness" is ultimately the power which doth

"preserve the stars from wrong,
And the most ancient heavens through it are fresh and strong."

Morality becomes consciously religious only when it becomes a voluntary energy of devotion to the eternal order of the universe. Let a man's heart really quicken with those sentiments of awe and wonder, gratitude and trust — which are so deeply implicated, not only in the scientific apprehension of the universe, but, indeed, in any simply human or poetic vision of its infinite perfections — and how can he help desiring, longing, steadfastly resolving to give himself in earnest service of that infinite power whose manifestations have awakened in him all these sentiments? So piety becomes enthusiasm for humanity. The one life is in every thing. There is nothing without it. And all things are for every one. Just as the heavens globe themselves in every drop of dew, so does the universe in every individual life. All that has ever been was preparation for this infinitesimal life of yours and mine. All the pasts help us; all the futures beckon us. And now what is the natural, the inevitable response of any heart that feels all this: that all is so for each; that one, the Infinite, is so for all.

What can it be but Each for all; each for the Infinite One? And this is morality with a divine emphasis. Such morality, so crowned and glorified, no one can doubt, is a true part of religion.

Whatever substitutes for religion have been, or may yet be invented, that only has a perfect right to be considered a factor of religion which has been vitally associated with it from the earliest times. Evolution may exalt and purify the contents of religion, but the contents thus exalted and purified must not be dissipated into viewless air. And as morality has always been so vitally associated with religion that the scope of evolution must continue to embrace its sacred trusts, so has the idea of another life been so vitally associated with it that the scope of evolution in the future cannot be exclusive of its tender radiance or solemn beauty. Certainly there have been great developments of religion of which the conviction of another life has been no part (Judaism, for example), or upon which the thought (as in the case of Buddhism), so far from being joyful and inspiring, lay like the weight of mountains. But special circumstances induced both of these exceptions to the rule, which is, that the idea of a future life has been included in the data of religion, as one of the most prominent, from the beginning of religion until now. The doctrine of immortality is older than the doctrine of the gods, — was its progenitor, as we have seen. And so I cannot help thinking that the scope of religious evolution in the future must be inclusive of this idea. With the decay of proofs once thought to be sufficient, there may be less of confident assertion, less of unwavering faith; but the idea need not be the less religious upon this account. A tender hope, deepening into serene assurance in great hours of thought, or in moments of unutterable love, — a perfect confidence that only that which is best for us as "members one of another" awaits us at the end; so long as these remain, the line of evolution cannot be said to be broken, and these may well be more religious in their implications than the most absolute dogmatism that deals in pocket-maps and vital statistics of the New Jerusalem.

However this may be, one thing is certain: this, that the future of religious evolution must include the element of worship, and the object of this worship must be no substitute for the Eternal, be it collective humanity or the moral ideal, but still the Eternal, the Infinite, "in whom we live and move and have our being." More silent than their fathers concerning him whom they call God, not speaking of him "as if he were a man on the next street," not parcelling out his attributes, not chattering about what he determined in the most secret counsels of the Trinity before the beginning of time, a tenderer awe, a holier reverence, shall be awakened by men's thought of him in coming times than ever in the past.

It may be that some of you will think me inconsistent here with what I said last Sunday morning. Then I insisted that the most vital essence of religion is not involved in a man's theory of God or Immortality, but in the awe which falls upon his mind as he confronts the universal order, and in the voluntary energy of self-surrender to this order which this awe inspires. If I had said or thought that the most vital essence of religion was merely some pleasant titillation consequent on seeing a glorious sunset or a pretty face, then there *would* be some inconsistency between what I said then and the emphasis which I now place upon the sense of a relation to the Infinite Power. But what I had in mind, and what I endeavored to express, was that no mere satisfaction or delight in isolated objects is vitally religious, but the awe and gladness which are quickened in us when this or that isolated experience suddenly opens out into all the infinities and immensities and eternities. Though it were Büchner himself, the boldest of materialists, who thrilled with this emotion, in spite of his philosophy he would then and there commune with an infinite spirit; his "tendency of matter to combine" would flash upon him as the Power, called by whatever name, adequate to produce the length and breadth and height and depth and beauty and sublimity and joy and love of this illimitable universe, and he would stand abashed and silent, if he did not like wondering Linnæus fall upon his knees. The most vital essence of religion *does* inhere in man's relation to the universe, but, however unconsciously, this relation, when it is at its best, implies a relation to a power which manifests itself in the totality of universal life and law. It is no mere aggregation of phenomena that inspires our awe. No, but the blending of their various chords into that harmony which we affirm as often as we say the universe, — the turned-into-one. To have this vision and the attendant consecration is indeed the most essential thing, but happiest of all are they who, consciously, can lift their hearts above all outward things to One who is the unseen Power, whose flowing garment the time-spirit is for ever weaving, the inmost thought and life and love, for ever baffling our comprehension, whom still our very ignorance affirms, for whom no name is adequate; whom, therefore, because we must still somehow speak of him, we call by the most simple name of all, a name which is no definition, but a continent for all the awe and reverence and adoration with which our hearts expand, — a name which we have spoken thousands of times, but which, now that we pause and think of it we hardly dare to speak at all, — and yet will speak, I with my lips, you in your silent hearts, — now let us speak it, — *God*.

JANUARY 12, 1879.

THE FAITH OF REASON.

HIM who dare name,
And yet proclaim,
Yes, I believe?
Who that can feel
His heart can steel
To say, I disbelieve?
GOETHE.

WHAT were the God who sat outside to scan
The spheres that 'neath his finger circling ran?
God dwells within, and moves the world and moulds,
Himself and Nature in one form enfolds.
GOETHE.

Mother of man's time-travelling generations,
    Breath of his nostrils, heart-blood of his heart,
God above all gods worshipped of all nations,
    Light above light, law beyond law, Thou art.
SWINBURNE.

III.

CONCERNING GOD.

CERTAINLY, it is not with any expectation of satisfying you or myself with what I have to say this morning concerning the highest of all themes that I venture to approach it, and invite your company. My treatment of this theme, as every man's, must be inadequate. The wisest here, however satisfactory they may be to others, will not be so to themselves. They will be less so in the future than they have been in the past. As knowledge widens with the lapse of time, less and less satisfactory will be men's speech concerning God. Language does not keep pace with thought and feeling. Two or three thousand, and even two or three hundred, years ago men had but little difficulty in finding words to express all they knew, or thought they knew, about God. Now it is different. The wisest lay a hushing finger on their lips.

> "Thought is deeper than all speech,
>   Feeling deeper than all thought;
> Souls to souls can never teach
>   What unto themselves is taught."

Meantime the air is thick with talk of atheism, with doleful prophecies and dreadful warnings. With the spread of atheism we are assured there will be a fearful moral revolution. Men will seek evil and pursue it. They have done right so far, because they have felt God's eye to be upon them, or because they have expected to give an account of their actions in another world. Such is the doctrine ; and, if it is true to any great extent, it would seem that there must follow some enfeeblement of the moral life. But it may be doubted whether the efficacy of the fear of hell as "a hangman's whip to hold the wretch in order," has not of late been overrated, and equally the dread of God's omniscience. It may also be doubted whether there is as much real atheism in the community as our terrorists insist. Men are silent or speak little, because any thing they can say seems so inadequate to express the sense of mystery which presses on their hearts. Many who are considered atheists do not consider themselves so, although they may prefer being considered so to having their attitude confounded with that of the majority. What they object to is not so much belief as definition. When Joubert says, "It is not a difficult matter to believe in God, if we are not asked to define him," it is not that he would be at liberty to believe in him as little as possible, but because he would be left free to expand his thought and feeling without bound; because *de*fined is *con*fined. So, too, when Matthew Arnold says: "We, too, would say God if the moment we said God you would not pretend that you know all about him." The majority of atheists are men whose thought and feeling about God transcend all ordinary statements, all popular definitions. Henry Thoreau said, "It would seem as if Atheism must be comparatively popular with God." Why, but because the so-called atheists are often men who reverence God too much to waste much time with any of the theologians. It is not to be denied, however, that there are those who not only consider themselves atheists, but wish to be considered so by others, insisting that they have no right to claim immunity from any odium which properly attaches to this designation. But this, in many cases, is only a concession of the right of the majority to determine the significance of words. In others it is a sort of vanity. In perfect frankness, it must be allowed that there are those in every community who consider *atheism* something *smart*. The satisfaction which such persons take in their atheism implies the God whom they deny. He must exist in order that they may have the distinction of saying to him, " Don't flatter yourself: *we* do not believe in you." Their imagination affirms him in order that their vanity may have the satisfaction of denying him to his face. But among earnest, thoughtful men real atheism is so rare a bird, that few have ever seen its raven plumage or heard the utter melancholy of its cry.

> "Man cannot be God's outlaw if he would;
> Nor so abscond him in the caves of sense
> But nature shall still search some crevice out
> With messages of splendor from that source
> Which soar he, dive he, baffles still and lures."

Even the would-be materialist, of the most unqualified stamp, who insists that there is but one substance in the world, and that this one substance is matter, only succeeds in spelling the name of his deity with six letters instead of three: M-a-t-t-e-r, instead of G-o-d. For, as Tyndall long ago declared, "If life and thought are the very flower of matter, any definition of matter which omits life and thought must be inadequate if not untrue." "No man has seen God at any time," says the New Testament. And this is just as true of him if you spell his name with six letters as if you spell it with three. No man has seen Matter at any time. Emerson is hardly less God-intoxicated than Spinoza, and yet his saying, "The divinity is in the atoms," is only a more poetic and impressive form of Büchner's suicidal confession that matter as such has "a tendency to combine."

The silence of some men concerning God seems to me vastly more reverent than the garrulity of others. Here a nameless thought, and there a multitude of words. Thoreau's idea, about atheism being comparatively popular with God, was also Plutarch's, who expressed it with greater fulness. "I, for my own part," he said, "had much rather men should say that there is not, and never was, any such person as Plutarch, than that they should say Plutarch is an unsteady, fickle, froward, vindictive, and touchy fellow." And so he inferred that God would rather have men deny his existence, than speak of him as unsteady, fickle, and so on. But then Plutarch was a pagan, and had pagan deities in mind. Christians would not, perhaps, be open to such criticism. They never represent their God as unsteady, fickle, or vindictive. Certainly not! But Plutarch's simile assumes that God is not the actual of the popular ideal. Were he the actual of Calvin's, I can fancy he would still appreciate the refusal of a man to believe him to be this, at its just value, even as a mortal man, although a conscious knave, would still appreciate a neighbor's misplaced confidence in his veracity and honor. Meantime, in my humble judgment, there is more of real reverence in six lines of Goethe than in all the creeds of all the sects: —

> "Him who dare name
> And yet proclaim,
> Yes, I believe?
> Who that can feel
> His heart can steel
> To say, I disbelieve?"

"Can man by searching find out God?" asks the Old Testament; and the New Testament of modern science repeats the question with an accent of yet deeper sadness. But our case is not so pitiful as it would be if God did not find *us* out whether we search for him or no. The most that all our searching does is generally to find, not God, but some excuse or reason for the ineradicable faith in him which is implanted in the most of us so deeply that I do not wonder that many have mistaken it for a primitive datum of consciousness. I doubt if any man ever consciously argued himself, or was argued into any real faith in God, — into aught more than some skin-deep belief in him. Faith in God is literally "the faith that is in us." How came it there? By supernatural revelation, says the supernaturalist. But revelation presupposes a revealer. Faith in a revelation presupposes faith in God. For the message to be sent, there must be a sender. For the message to be completely trusted, it must be impossible for God to lie. Moreover, with the advance of knowledge it becomes more and more unlikely that there has ever been any such thing as supernatural revelation. The genesis of the belief, common to all religions, is easily accounted for without the intervention of a single supernatural fact. The argument of Hume: "It is more likely that evidence should be false than that a miracle should be true," has never yet been proved fallacious, and grows in strength as men more clearly recognize that evidence, in order to be false, need not be consciously so. To evade the force of this argument by admitting that the miracle is natural, is to discharge the miracle of all authoritative significance. It must be supernatural in order to be invested with a divine authority. But if "the faith which is in us" — in the most of us, surely — did not come by revelation, how does it come? Theodore Parker used to say by consciousness. But the philosophers assure us that we can be conscious only of the affections of our mind. We cannot be conscious of that by which they are affected. Consciousness of God is then impossible. Again, it is affirmed, that "the faith which is in us" is an intuition. But what is an intuition? A necessary truth, answers the transcendentalist, — a necessary truth perceived by the reason without any assistance from the understanding. But intuitions of this sort do not enjoy the high repute to-day which they did formerly. It begins to be doubted whether there are any such intuitions; whether the mind can be split up into reason and understanding, or, at least, whether — to parody a saying of Herbert Spencer's — "expression is feature in the making" — the understanding is not reason in the making. The philosophy of experience inclines to the opinion that even "necessary truths" are discovered to be such by observation and experiment and reflection, that they do not inhere in mind as such. This philosophy also talks of intuitions, but its intuitions are not like those of the transcendentalist, — a kind of *super-rational* revelation privately communicated to each individual soul. They are the products of ancestral and race-experience organized in us. Our faith in God, then, is an intuition, — the flower of an hereditary experience, whose roots are buried in an immemorial past. Thanks for its beauty and its fragrance, as it opens in the hushed seclusions of our hearts! But evidently an intuition of this sort, a product of experience, can have no such authority as would the intuition of the transcendentalist if this were all which it was formerly conceived to be. Some, indeed, may be so constituted that they can enjoy the great inheritance on which they enter here, without ever thinking or wondering how it came to them, and whether it is lawfully theirs. The majority are, in fact, so constituted. But there are not a few who, once they know that the faith which is in them is no supernatural gift, no organic necessity, but an inheritance from the past, must set about to find the title-deeds, must know, if possible, how the estate was earned; what work was done, what battles fought, before it was entailed to them. This is the meaning of a world of patient study in these latter days into the origin and development of men's religious ideas. Tylor, and Spencer, and Coulange, and Lubbock, and the rest, what are they but patient searchers of our title-deeds, in order that we may know whether our right is indefeasible in this estate of faith in God which has come down to us from immemorial times? Honor to those who, finding themselves unable to make out their title to their own satisfaction, vacate the premises; albeit for them to do so is to go forth like Abraham, not knowing whither! For such also, believe me, there is "a city that hath foundations." But happy they who dare believe that their inheritance, however dubious the title of their remotest ancestors, has in the course of centuries been fairly earned; and that, when superstition's every lien upon it has been discharged, it will still be ample for the free soul to revel and rejoice in, without fear of any interdict of science or any challenge that the lords of reason can oppose to her possession!

It cannot be denied that an element of unreality enters very largely into the primitive idea of God, if the genesis of this idea has been correctly made out by the most learned anthropologists and sociologists. There are those who think that when the genesis of this idea has been shown to be involved in misconceptions almost innumerable, the idea has itself been relegated to the sphere of childish superstition. If the phenomena of sleep and trance first suggested to mankind the idea of "an inner man"—a soul; if the analogy of sleep and death suggested that the soul was still alive when its "last sleep" had settled on the body; if the ancestral ghosts thus arrived at, from being at first regarded as mere human ghosts to be invoked, placated, and so on, came at length to be regarded as gods, the ghost-food passing over into sacrifice, the invocations into prayers; if, further on, stones and trees, then clouds, and heat and cold, and wind, and sun and moon and stars,—all came to be regarded as the seats of ghostly power; if this is a correct interpretation of the phenomena of primitive religion, does not the idea of God engendered in this ghostly atmosphere become itself as "thin as a ghost"? How from the midst of so much unreality could ever come by any legitimate process the idea of that Supreme Reality which we of modern times mean to suggest as often as we speak of God?

My answer is that, if the beginning of the God-idea was such as I have tried to indicate,—and I believe that it was so,—we ought not to confound the essence of the feeling out of which it came with their rational psychology with which it was associated. The essence of the feeling was a sense of the mysteriousness of human life. That which oppressed the primitive man with awe and wonder was essentially the same fact before which our latest science stands abashed, — the connection between mind and body. It was the mystery attaching to the thought of ghostly ancestors, peopling the forest-haunts with shadowy denizens, that made it possible for the sentiment of worship to go out to them from the poor savage heart; and, however trivial the psychology, the mystery was real enough; so that to say that the first step in the evolution of the God-idea was unreal is to mistake its formal accident for its essential character. And so, further along, grant that the indwelling life ascribed to tree or stone, which constituted these objects fetiches, or to sun and moon and stars in the next stage, which we call nature-worship; grant that this indwelling life was made up, to the imagination of the savage, of one or more of the great company of ghosts which, by this time had quite forgotten, as it were, their human relations, — the fact remains that, antecedent to this theory of ghostly life, there must have been the sense of life to be accounted for. What the savage did was to account for it by the only life with which he felt himself to be acquainted. His intentions were excellent. He thought he was proceeding from the known to the unknown. In the strictest sense, it may be said that the God-idea was not fairly born until the world of ghosts had gradually become a vast mysterious realm of life, an incalculable store of energy on which the savage mind could draw in order to account for any natural phenomenon that appealed to it for a solution of the mystery of its seeming life. The key of his position, meanwhile, was his sense of seeming life to be accounted for. The god he really worshipped was this seeming life. His ghostly explanation was, no doubt, entirely insufficient. But it was not his explanation that he worshipped. It was the seeming life which he endeavored to explain.

The next step beyond nature-worship in the development of the God-idea was polytheism; the worship of many gods, not in objective forms as in fetichism and nature-worship, but as imaginary beings, whose genesis is to be accounted for in various ways. As the phenomena of nature and society were rudely classified, a single spirit was imagined as the controlling deity of each separate class. The choice of this deity was variously determined. "To him that hath shall be given," was a controlling principle. As the big fish eat up the little ones, so the big gods devoured their smaller rivals. The favorite gods of nature-worship became the gods of polytheism, to the exclusion of their less significant companions. Another source of income to the polytheistic pantheon was the apotheosis of distinguished chiefs, warriors, medicine-men, and so on, for whom the attributes of the nature-myths had a remarkable affinity. But in this polytheistic stage of the God-idea the noticeable thing is this, that what was really worshipped was the hidden life which was the background of phenomenal existence. The gods of polytheism were but so many explanations of this life, then the most reasonable that could be had. But the real object of worship was the hidden life; the Power that made the trees wave and the waters flow, the sun and moon and stars to shine, the earth to rise out of her wintry grave clad in the spring-time beauty. The only unreality was in the explanation. The mystery which polytheism endeavored to explain was *a bond fide* mystery. It might well make men's hearts tremble with fear, or swell with rapture, or dilate with joy.

From polytheism, the worship of many gods, to monotheism, the worship of one, was the next step in the development of the God-idea. Here also the principle, "To him that hath shall be given," had, no doubt, great influence. The favorite god tended to be the only one, little by little crowding the others from their thrones. Different tribes had different favorites, and the strongest tribe demanded exclusive worship for its deity, and was able to enforce the claim. Natural selection operated here as in the physical world. There was a struggle for existence, and a preservation of the fittest; the fittest here not meaning the best, but, as often in the physical world, only the strongest; the ablest to survive. Midway between polytheism and monotheism we have monolatry, the exclusive worship of one deity without denying the existence of others. But gods not worshipped cease to be regarded as realities. The god exclusively worshipped tends to be the only god to whom existence is allowed. And hence a monotheistic God-idea.

At this stage of development, as at every earlier, it must be admitted that there are elements of unreality involved in every step of the advance. But here again, as at every previous stage, the unreality was in the explanation, not in the thing explained. The real object of worship here, as before, was the mystery of life behind phenomena. The dawning sense of unity in these, the beginning of all science and philosophy, suggested the unity of the underlying mystery. I grant you that the monotheistic god was at first dreadfully anthropomorphic: "a non-natural man," "a man of war;" to the Semite a Bedouin sheik at first, and then a king,— the earthly monarchy always tending to produce a heavenly counterpart in human thought. But, again, the noticeable thing is that the real object of awe and wonder and worship was not the man-like deity,— that he was not reverenced and worshipped for his man-likeness, but as the mysterious Power adequate to produce the world of nature and humanity. The man-likeness was a necessity of childish thought, of undevelopment, of survival in culture; but it could not successfully impeach the reality of the Mysterious Power of which it was the concrete symbol, nor the reality of the worship honestly accorded to this Power.

With the development of monotheism, the God-idea reaches its highest point of evolution, except as this idea once generated is capable of indefinite purification. And the most notable feature in this process is the transference of man's awe and wonder from the exceptional in his experience to the regular and orderly. From the lowest fetich-worshipper up to the average Christian monotheist of this nineteenth century, the most potent suggestions of deity have come from the apparently exceptional and abnormal. The disposition of the untutored savage to choose for his fetich the most grotesque object — tree or stone — that he can find, is absolutely identical with the disposition of the cultured modern Christian to seek for God in some miraculous interposition rather than in the invariable order of the world, "staring with wonder to see water turned into wine, and heedless of the stupendous fact of his own personality." So pertinacious has been the resolution of the religious world to find God only in the apparently abnormal and inconsequent, that, by force of association, it came at length to be regarded as an axiom that, if God is not a sort of "prince of misrule," then he is nothing. Parallel with the development of religion for hundreds of years, there has been a development of science. But the tendency of science has been to everywhere dissipate the wonder inhering in the apparently abnormal and inconsequent by including them in its generalizations of law and order. Sure of his axiom, "The more law the less God;" the religionist has contemplated this process with unqualified dismay. Province after province has been wrested from the domain of personal agency and annexed to the domain of law, till it has seemed only a question of time whether every vestige of the Deity would not finally be expelled from the universe. But while, little by little, the old sense of mystery, inhering in the apparently exceptional and abnormal, has been going out, a new sense of mystery, slowly but surely has been coming in, — a sense of mystery inhering in the uniformities of natural phenomena. The more law, the more God — the more mystery, wonder, awe, and trust — has been the growing conviction which has kept pace with this development. "As fast as science transfers more and more things from the category of irregularities to the category of regularities, the mystery that once attached to the superstitious explanation of them becomes a mystery attaching to the scientific explanation of them; there is a merging of many special mysteries in one general mystery."[1] "So that," says Herbert Spencer, "beginning with the germinal idea of mystery which the savage gets from a display of [anomalous] power, . . . and the germinal sentiment of awe accompanying it, the progress is towards an ultimate recognition of a mystery

---

[1] Spencer's Study of Sociology, p. 310.

behind every act and appearance, and a transfer of the awe from something special and occasional to something universal and unceasing;" which something is the infinite God of scientific faith.

If now I have accomplished my purpose, I have made it plain that no unreality attaching to the earliest development of religion, or to any subsequent stage, has prejudiced the value of the God-idea in its present form or indeed in any form it has assumed from the beginning of its long and painful march from puerile animism up to the glorious consciousness of One who,

> "be he what he may,
> Is yet the fountain light of all our day,
> Is yet the master-light of all our seeing."

This has been proved by showing that, at every stage, a *bonâ fide* mystery has been involved in the idea; and that the real object of awe and reverence and worship has been this mystery, and not the explanation of it, varying with every stage of culture.

How then? Do I erect an altar "to the unknown God," and bid you come and worship? I answer Yes and No. "Unknown and yet well known" is a Pauline phrase with which we may complement the inscription which the apostle found on the Athenian altar. *Unknown and yet well known!* A friend suggests to me, "The Sum of the Unknown" as the best possible definition of God, a definition which neither defines nor confines. Such a definition would indefinitely postpone the advent of atheism; for, though "the sum of the unknown" is being steadily abridged by the discoveries of science, there is no immediate danger of its being wholly conquered and annexed to the domain of knowledge. And then, too, while "the sum of the unknown" is always growing smaller, it is always growing larger to our apprehension. The more we know, the better do we realize what realms of mystery, still unexplored, challenge our patience and our courage. But, remote as is the possibility, I do not relish the idea that, if we could know every thing, we could write God's epitaph; that the increase of knowledge is a gradual elimination of the unknown quantity, God, from the equation of our thought and feeling. Moreover, the unknown which has elicited the awe and reverence of men's hearts has never been a simple negative. It has been wonderful to them and awful and reverend as the mysterious background of something known or felt to be so. And, with the advance of science, what makes the ever vaster amplitude of the unknown so quickening to our awe, our gladness, and our trust, is that the little we do know is so wonderful, so marvellous; and we proceed to people all the vast unknown with the benignant forms and forces which have been openly revealed to us. It is as when I stand upon the rocky headlands of my native shore, and look out upon that "glorious mirror where the Almighty's form glasses itself in tempests."

> "Eastward as far as the eye can see,
> Eastward, eastward, endlessly,
> The sparkle and tremor of purple sea."

Surely what fills me with a joy so keen that it is almost pain is not alone the flashing tumult of the great expanse of waters; it is also that, beyond where sky and water meet, with my mind's eye I see the mighty ocean reaching on and on, and beautiful with the same unspeakable beauty as the little space that lies within my field of vision. It is the beauty of the known that makes the beauty of the unknown so sure and so entrancing. And just as surely my soul's "normal delight in the infinite God" is not produced by any purely negative unknown. No more is it by any positive known. No, but by my warrantable conviction that all the infinite unknown is equally with the little territory which I know the haunt of nameless beauty, order, symmetry, and law. And so to those among us, and they are not few, who are endeavoring to convince us that a purely negative mystery, an absolute unknown, is adequate to all the functions of a God whom we may reverence and adore, I answer in the words of England's greatest living theologian: "Far be it

"from us to deal lightly with the sense of mys-
"tery. It mingles largely with all devout appre-
"hension, and is the great redeeming power that
"purifies the intellect of its egotism and the heart
"of its pride. But you cannot constitute a reli-
"gion out of mystery alone, any more than out of
"knowledge alone, nor can you measure the re-
"lation of doctrines to humility and piety by the
"mere amount of conscious darkness that they
"leave. All worship, being directed to what is
"above us and transcends our comprehension,
"stands in the presence of a mystery. But not
"all that stands before a mystery is worship.
"The abyss must not be one of total gloom —
"of neutral possibilities — of hidden glories or
"hidden horrors, we know not which. . . . Such
"a pit of indeterminate contingencies will bend
"no head, and melt no eye that may turn to it.
"Some rays of clear light must escape from
"it, some visions of solemn beauty gleam within
"it, ere the darkness itself can be 'visible'
"enough to deliver its awfulness upon the
"soul. . . . To fling us into bottomless nega-

"tion is to drown us in mystery and leave us
"dead. True reverence can breathe and see,
"only on condition of some alternation of light
"and darkness, of inner silence and a stir of
"upper air."

Nor is there any thing in the necessities of the most rigid scientific thought which violates this condition; which precludes this happy alternation. "Though unknown, yet well known." Is he not this, — the God of scientific apprehension? In any scientific sense, it must be granted that in himself he is unknown, unknowable; and must remain so always. But until I can know some one thing in the universe *in itself*, be that thing clod of earth or soul of man, I will not fret because I cannot know in itself the Infinite and Everlasting One. For what does my ignorance signify but that an unmanifested infinite can never be found out; that an everlasting silence would be totally inaudible? "Vapid words," we say with Martineau, "in a universe full of visions and of voices!"

Meanwhile, though I acknowledge, unreservedly, that the unspeakable majesty is in itself unknown, I insist that our ignorance should not, cannot be interpreted as describing absolute nonentity of perception and apprehension. Our very ignorance affirms the existence of an incomprehensible substance of which the phenomenal universe is the perpetual manifestation. Our knowledge of God is of exactly the same nature as our knowledge of our neighbors and ourselves. We know him by the manifestations of his inscrutable life. If we are not so garrulous as men were formerly about his attributes, we know a great deal more about his laws, the habits of his infinite life. What he determined in the most secret counsels of the Trinity before the beginning of time, the Calvins and the Edwardses have sufficiently discussed; and all who care for their results are welcome to embrace them. What we are sure of is, that the Unseen Power was adequate to the production of this universe, such as it is. He has put himself into his world as painters sometimes put themselves into their pictures; not by painting himself, like

Raphael, in a corner, but by expressing his stupendous energy in every part. As much as we know of the universe, so much we know of God. Truly it is not much in comparison with what we do not know. " Lo, these are parts of his ways, but how little is yet known of him." And yet, though relatively little, absolutely much, and more with every new discovery of any fact or law. Now, indeed, for the first time Theology makes good her boast, *Scientia scientiarum*, the science of sciences; but not in the old sense of being superior to all others, rather in the sense of including all others. Henceforth all other sciences are fragments of theology; for all of them are busy with the manifestations of the one eternal substance in which all phenomena inhere.

Modern science is unitarian, monotheistic, as never was the creed of Moses or Mohammed. She teaches us that all these nerves whose play upon the surface of the universe irradiate it with such various expression go back into one central ganglion, and ever more report its perfect sanity. From all the peaks, from all the depths and heights, the different forms and forces of the world are signalling across to one another with fraternal salutations. A thousand and ten thousand various lines of force run back into one central stream whose ceaseless energy supplies them all. What was the wonder of that old *homöousion*, — *one* substance of the Son and Father, a barren abstraction, — to this *homoiousion*, *like* substance of all worlds, which modern astronomy has proved? From every quarter comes the news of this same unity and sympathy and harmony in the make of things. "It thunders all around." A universal solidarity bespeaks a central and abiding Oneness at the heart of things.

Whether the infinite power, the infinite life, is personal or impersonal, is one of the questions about which those who are least qualified to speak are the most voluble. Can any one of them tell us what personality is? And till they can what right have they to say, "A god who is not personal is no god at all." The first use of this word person, which is from *per* and *sono* and means to sound through, was to designate one sounding through a mask the dramatic situations of some poet's verse. And as in the the great amphitheatre at Athens, the person and poet were sometimes the same, — even Sophocles speaking from behind the mask his own majestic words, — so always in this amphitheatre whose circle is the circle of the universe, the person and the poet are one: it is his own poem, neither tragedy nor comedy, but an epic which includes them both, and many a lyric passage of sweetness unimaginable till heard, that the Infinite recites, less, it may be, for our delight than because irresistibly self-stirred to self-expression. But, I am well aware, the sticklers for personality will not be put off with any such metaphor as this. If only we could all agree upon the meaning of personality, there might be less divergence in our thought than there is now. With some a person is an individual, a local deity. Such expect to see God when they die, and to recognize him by his resemblance to the conventional portraiture of Jesus, unaware that this is based upon an antique bust of Plato, which for a long time was supposed to be a bust of Christ. Many who declare that they do not believe in a personal god mean little more than that they do not believe in any such individual god as this in any localized deity. But many who insist that God is personal are far enough from this pathetic puerility. What they mean by personality is conscious mind, or simply mind. The new psychology is making it a little easier for us to conceive of personality in this sense, as universally diffused. It refuses to locate the thinking apparatus solely in the brain. Rather every part of us seems to think or at least to be concerned in thinking.

> "Her pure and eloquent blood
> Spoke in her cheeks, and so distinctly wrought
> That one might almost say her body thought."

So it becomes a little easier to conceive of infinite mind, of infinite thought and will, not here or there, but all-pervading. In this sense, shall we then say that God is personal? Or shall we rather say that mind and thought and will and love, all personal words, are the least inadequate symbols that we have, or can have, of the Infinite Power, and try, always, to remember that they are symbols, not exact expressions for that which cannot be expressed? "God's thoughts are not our thoughts; neither are his ways our ways." This is a real prophetic word, — prophetic of our wisest modern thought. Only let us not forget what follows: "For as the heavens are higher than the earth, so are his thoughts higher than our thoughts and his ways than our ways." There are those who seem to think that to deny personality to God is to assert that he is something less than personal. And with the materialist, if there be any such, who really imagines that out of mere dead matter without any God-like energy behind it came this sublime and awful universe, the denial of personality to God may be to affirm that he is something less than personal. But this sort of a materialist is hard to find. He has only a verbal existence. My friend assures me we are looking up over our heads for an explanation which we should look for down under our feet. But no. If matter is the ultimate reality, then matter is not down under our feet, but up over our heads. The less does not produce the greater. There is an infinite element involved in every step of evolution. The ascending series can be accounted for only by supposing a higher than its highest, antecedent to its lowest term. But to deny personality to God is not necessarily to affirm that he is something less than personal. It may be to affirm that he is infinitely more. There are those who think the Infinite altogether such an one as themselves, as Caliban his " dam's god, Setebos," and such regard with pity and contempt, because they cannot say that God is personal, men who have each one of them religion enough to set up a whole army of their assailants. But there are those who cannot say that God is personal, because they dare not apply to the Eternal the limitations of our human personality. Not because they conceive of God as less than personal, but because they conceive of him as infinitely more, do they decline to call him so. If they were sure their words would be accepted as symbolical, then they might say, as I do, that personality is a far better symbol than impersonality of the inexpressible fact.

But I should do injustice to those who contend most wisely and acutely for the idea of infinite personality, if I did not make haste to say that it is possible for these, as well as for their opponents, to affirm that God is more than personal. To affirm personality is not necessarily to affirm that this designation is exhaustive of the fulness of the infinite life. It is only to affirm that there are manifestations of this life which compel this designation in the absence of a better. There may, at the same time, be other manifestations, incalculably vast, which demand either a different designation, or that silence which is golden. This should not be forgotten. It is, too often, by those who refuse to speak of God as personal because he is to them more than personal. He may be more than personal to those who affirm his personality with the utmost confidence.

The idea of consciousness, as included in the idea of personality, is often felt, on the one hand, to be the greatest stumbling-block, and, on the other, to be the most absolute desideratum. In the latter case is not the tendency conspicuous to make the Infinite "altogether such an one as ourselves"? Yet, though I do not see that the alternative of consciousness is "a blind force," that bugbear of the popular theology, one thing, at least, is certain, — that the non-ability to scientifically discover consciousness in the universe is no sign it is not there, nor even a hint that it is not. We are so sure of nothing else as of our own consciousness, and yet what scientific evidence have we of its existence? Not a particle. The saying of Lawrence that his scalpel found no soul in the brain has been thought by would-be atheists a confirmation of La Place's saying that his telescope, scanning the whole heavens, found no trace of God. In fact it negatives it altogether. If the scalpel had found a soul, we might perhaps expect the telescope to find a God. The fact that it has not, while still we know that it exists, establishes a vast presumption in favor of a universal mind. But if an infinite mind, says Du Bois Reymond, then too an infinite brain. Well, one of the atomic philosophers has said that, if we could see the dance of atoms, it would be not unlike the dance of constellations. Whereupon, Mr. Martineau turns round upon Reymond, and says: "If the structure and movement of atoms "do but repeat in little those of the heavens, what "hinders us from inverting the analogy, and say-"ing that the ordered heavens repeat the rhythm "of the cerebral particles? You need an em-"bodied mind? Lift up your eyes and look upon "the arch of night as the brow of the Eternal, its "constellations as the molecules of the universal "consciousness and its ethereal waves as media "of omniscient thought." As an *argumentum ad hominem* this could not be better, but Mr. Martineau knows as well as anybody that once sure of such a cosmic brain the philosophers would immediately attribute it to "some cosmic megatherium," not to the great first cause. Doubtless if this is conscious, its consciousness like gravitation reports itself at every point, and is not central but ubiquitous. Enough that infinite consciousness can never be disproved, and that, if there be no such consciousness, then there is something better, else could it never be in us.

If it could be generally understood that the language of religion is not scientific but poetical, we might freely make use of various expressions which now it seems almost our duty to avoid; we might, for example, speak of the creation of the world and of God as the Creator, as naturally as we now speak of the sun's rising and setting, although we know our words entirely fail to represent the fact. "In the beginning God created the heavens and the earth?" Then the beginning is not over yet, for he is still at work upon his world. The old doctrine of creation pictured an eternal being, dwelling in loneliness until about six thousand years ago, when suddenly he awoke and became active, created matter out of nothing, and the universe out of matter, and then relapsed again into quiescence. Harried by geologist and astronomer, the expounders of this scheme agreed to interpret liberally the six days of creation, and put back the beginning to some infinitely distant past. But no such concession can relieve the scheme of its essential incoherence and absurdity. Philosophy opposes its incorrigible *ex nihilo nihil* — nothing from nothing — and science brings a thousand arguments to prove the indestructibility and consequent eternity of matter. The conception of matter as a "datum objective to God," a finite substance lying over against his infinite, is inconceivably absurd. It but remains for us to consider the material universe as in no sense foreign to God.

> "All are but parts of one stupendous whole,
> Whose body Nature is, and God the soul."

If this is Pantheism, it is no worse for being so. For in one form or another Pantheism has always been the doctrine of the most religious souls. The idea of a mechanical Creator coalesces at no single point with this conception. He was supposed to be outside the universe working upon it like a watchmaker at work upon a watch.

But the watch proves to be so big that there is no room outside of it, no outer darkness. "This thing was not done in a corner."

> "God dwells in all, and moves the world, and moulds,
> Himself and Nature in one form enfolds."

This is the new doctrine of creation. Only it is not creation. It is evolution. God is no builder, no architect, no infinite mechanician. A rose upon its stem in June is a more adequate symbol of his unfolding life than any Christopher Wren or Michael Angelo. From within outwards, not from without inwards, is the procession of the Holy Spirit.

> "The flower horizons open,
> The blossom vaster shows,
> We hear the wide worlds echo,
> 'See how the lily grows!'"

Friends, I have kept you long; and still I have a hundred things to say. But they will keep against another time. The one thing I have tried to do this morning is to clear the god-idea of that appearance of unreality which attaches to its earliest forms; to show you that at every step the unreality inhered not in the essence, but in the accidents of the idea; to show you that, as it has come down to us, it is no mere survival of an ancient superstition, but the legitimate product of men's enraptured recognition of the mysterious Power which manifests itself in all the marvellous uniformities of universal nature and life. Further than this, I have endeavored to turn a ray of light on some of the more prominent questions which are engaging the attention of the more thoughtful persons of our time; to show you that a purely negative mystery is by no means equal to the proper function of the God-idea, that it can rightfully demand no reverence, inspire no sacred awe, beget no holy trust; and, finally, to suggest that even such shibboleths as "personality" and "creation" can be pronounced sibboleth, or remain quite unspoken, and the protesting mind still entertain the God-idea in a more worthy form than that of its conventional exponents. But, after all that has been said, how infinitesimal it seems in contrast with the supreme idea it has sought to honor! O God, we thank thee that our joy and peace and satisfaction and delight in thee are not dependent on our ability to speak of thee aright; that deeper than all speech, all thought, the sense abides in us of thy ineffable mystery, thy glorious power, thy steadfast law, thine everlasting faithfulness, thy constant presence, and thy perfect love!

> "Thy voice is on the rolling air,
>   I hear thee where the waters run,
>   Thou standest in the rising sun,
> And in the setting thou art fair.
>
> "What art thou then? I cannot guess;
>   But though I seem in star and flower
>   To feel thee, some diffusive power,
> I do not therefore love thee less.
>
> "Far off thou art, but ever nigh;
>   I have thee still and I rejoice:
>   I prosper circled by thy voice;
> I shall not lose thee though I die."

JANUARY 19, 1879.

IV.

CONCERNING IMMORTALITY.

THE subject of my discourse this morning has been always and everywhere, almost without exception, one of engrossing interest. The literature of the subject is one of the most convincing evidences of this that can be shown. Some fifteen years ago Professor Ezra Abbot made a list of authors who had treated of the future life, and of their books. It contained between five and six thousand names and titles. The list was necessarily imperfect. Then, too, it was a list of books which still exist. As many more no doubt have sunk into an oblivion deeper than any bibliographer or bibliomaniac can go down. If more had done so, Professor Abbot's list would have been shorter, but the world would not have suffered by the loss. Again, if Professor Abbot's list had come down to 1879, it would have contained, perhaps, the names of twice as many authors and books. For never, I imagine, has the subject of Immortality been so fruitful of printed discussion as during the last dozen years. And yet, if we could have all the books that have ever been printed on this subject, and all that have not been printed,—doubtless a greater host,—and all the sermons that have been written upon it, and all the poems, like the stars in heaven for multitude, we should still have no adequate exponent of the interest humanity has taken in this theme. For this interest antedates the earliest literary expression by hundreds and thousands of years. Before the invention of the first rude alphabet, a ruder faith in immortality had stirred the savage heart alike with hope and fear. And, since the beginning of man's literary life, hundreds of millions who have never written sermon, or book, or poem, or even one poor word, have through their personal experience of loss and death, been led to wonder what could be the meaning of it all.

One of our modern sculptors has made an Eve and Abel, the ideal mother of humanity confronting for the first time the mysterious fact of death embodied in her child. What is the sleep from which no voice can waken ? Science forbids us to conceive any such newness and surprise of death as that. But art has never had a more suggestive theme. The genius of Michael Angelo could not have exhausted it. Yet the last mother would afford him a far better subject than the first. For death is not less wonderful to us than it was to our remotest ancestors. Nay, it is far more wonderful. Even the objective fact is different. That death should be the "end-all" of the primeval savage is conceivable. That it should be the end-all of Shakspere, of Socrates, of Jesus, — that is another matter. But the subjective power of wonder has undergone an equal if not greater change. And, taking subject and object together, surely never, since thought and death began their great career, has thought confronted death with such a look, — so full of earnest questioning — as that which now half shadows, half irradiates, the solemn beauty of her face.

But the subject is so closely implicated with men's personal experience, their sorrow for their dead, their individual hopes of a hereafter, in which love shall reunite its broken chain, that there is hardly any task from which the preacher would more willingly be exempt than the subjection of this matter to the impartial tests of reason and science. The multiplication of railroads in China is said to be hopelessly impeded by the veneration of the people for their graves. The engineer cannot cut through them; he must go round them, — a difficult matter in a land so full of graves. A similar difficulty meets the scientific thinker when he would deal with immortality. Somebody's grave is always in the way. Not to go straight ahead is to spoil his science, as for the engineer it is to spoil his road. But has he the heart to do it? Not often, it must be confessed. I have read hundreds of sermons and essays which set out to do so bravely enough, not one of which held straight on to the goal. As Milanion's golden apples arrested Atalanta's flying feet, so here the heart of some poor stricken one, lying there bleeding in the way, that must be taken up and stanched and soothed. But they are few who even propose to themselves to apply reason and science to this theme. The majority imagine that it does not come within their sphere, and some who are not of this majority are satisfied with presenting to their hearers a set of reasons for believing in a future life, not one of which has any weight *with them*, but which many of their hearers think entirely conclusive, simply because they have never had a doubt. I could do this this morning, and I could do it so adroitly that without committing myself I could give you the impression that to my own mind my set of reasons left nothing to be desired. But some of you would think me easily convinced, and I should think myself one of many who in these latter days defile the preacher's office with their appalling insincerity; "liars for God," not all of whom are "orthodox."

To speak one's frankest word concerning God may be less difficult than to speak it concerning immortality. For there are people who if they told you true would rather give up their belief in God than their belief in immortality. It is not that their dread of self-extinction is so great; but that some one has gone away from them whom they would climb to meet again, if need be, on the ruins of the universe. It is this fact which must make the doctrine ever venerable. It is the apotheosis of love. Whatever may have been the stronghold of this doctrine in times past, to-day it is the passionate tenderness of human hearts. It gives back the object of affection. A few may cling to it for other reasons. The majority cling to it for this alone. I know that there are those who allow that this is so, and *therefore* condemn the doctrine as utterly selfish. Ah, but the good desired, and which this faith assures, is not so much love-getting as love-giving! It is those who have given the most whose longing after immortality is most intense. Grant that there is nothing specially religious in such a longing. But there is something eternally beautiful; something which should speak to the most sceptical as they approach it, saying as the god said to Moses in the grand old Hebrew fable, "Take off thy shoes from off thy feet; for the spot whereon thou standest is holy ground."

It is not uncommon in these latter days to hear men speak of immortality as if the doctrine were essentially ignoble. But, to my mind, even if this doctrine could be shown to have no reasonableness whatever, it would still be, after the thought of God, the brightest crown which has adorned the brows of our humanity in all the past. Whatever else it has been, this doctrine has been the glorious symbol of man's self-respect; presumptuous perhaps, but better this than self-despising. I know well enough that the doctrine is not necessarily noble. A minister of the Established Church of Scotland has recently written, "However different the representations of heaven, they all agree in representing it as a state of gratified and glorified selfishness; of blessedness which appeals above all to selfish desire and selfish hope." A sweeping statement this; too sweeping to be true, and yet with an amount of truth in it that is terrible to think of. But let the worst that can be said with truth be said. Let all the meanness, all the superstition, and all the selfishness that have inhered in this doctrine, be charged against it. What an indictment it would be, and yet how far from exhausting the capacity or the historic significance of this doctrine! For what has kept the doctrine alive in spite of so much base interpretation is, that it has been the symbol of man's self-respect, self-reverence; the measure of his awe in the presence of his own intellectual and moral nature; and of his assurance that love is stronger than death. To represent this doctrine as necessarily or always selfish and ignoble, is to ignore some of the grandest chapters in the history of human nature. Taken at its worst, in ancient or in modern times, and there is nothing more contemptible than this same doctrine, of selfishness and meanness all compact. But, taken at its best, there is nothing more exalted and exalting. Prove it has no validity whatever, and it is still the peer of any star that ever sparkled in the firmament of thought. Prove it *the grand mistake*, and it is a mistake which reflects more honor on humanity than hundreds of its verifiable truths.

We are indebted to Frances Power Cobbe, I believe, for the phrase "magnanimous atheism." Corresponding to this phrase, there is a possible reality which may not be ignored. And as there is "magnanimous atheism," so there may be magnanimous doubt and even dogmatic denial of immortality, whose motto is,

"Is there no second life; pitch this one high."

But as all atheism is not magnanimous, so is not all doubt of immortality or all denial. There are those who plume themselves upon their disbelief, as if it were something very grand and fine to say, "I do not care to be immortal." But not to care to be immortal argues not greatness but littleness of mind. The magnanimous doubter or denier is the man who does care for it mightily, who resents with all the energy of his mind and heart the indignity of absolute annihilation, but who accepts his fate with courage, because it seems to him a necessary part of the beneficent order of the universe. Not *care* to be immortal? Have you ever thought, have you ever loved, have you ever worshipped, and can yet say this? I *do* care for it. Prove to me that I have no reason to believe in it or hope for it, and I will bear my fate as best I can. But I can never cease to care for it.

To give the reasons which men assign for their belief in immortality, is not to account for their belief, — its strength and permanence. Their reasons, for the most part, are not reasons, only excuses for an instinctive faith. That there is this instinctive faith is with some minds an argument for it that precludes the need of any other. And so long as this instinctive faith was regarded as a component part of the mind as such, not something acquired, and God was thought to be the maker of the mind, just as a man is the maker of a watch; so long it might very naturally be regarded as a proof of the objective reality of the immortal life. But what if the instinctive faith is but the last result of the faith of innumerable ancestors, a faith based upon reasons more or less fanciful? Such is the latest diagnosis of the psychologists. We organically inherit the faiths of the past, but not the reasons of the men of the past for holding these faiths. And not inheriting the reasons, we infer that the instinctive faiths are super-rational; ineradicable factors of the mind as such. Psychology dissipating this idea, and showing that present instinct is the product of past reason, it becomes the duty of every person who desires to live a rational, not merely an instinctive life, to bring his inherited instincts to the bar of present reason and see what they are worth. If the verdict is unfavorable, the instincts may still triumphantly assert themselves, and hence the contradiction of the head and heart noticeable in so many lives. The majority are satisfied with an instinctive life. That you are not is evident from your being here. If you are believing yourselves immortal because of some remote ancestor's childish philosophy of sleep and dreams, you want to know it. To wilfully cherish an illusion, known to be such, or even suspected of being such, may do for cowards. It will not do for honest and courageous men and women.

Consider, then, with me some of the reasons which have resulted in the instinctive faith of modern men in immortality. Apparently it was the analogy of sleep and death which first suggested to mankind the survival of the soul upon the cessation of the body from its ordinary functions. During the stillness of sleep, the soul was thought to be absent from the body and to waken it on its return. So when death's deeper stillness supervened, the soul was only thought to be away upon a longer journey, and all the care with which the lifeless form was cherished was inspired by the idea that it would some day be occupied again by its former tenant. For so many thousands of years did men live contentedly in this order of ideas that to this day the thought and speech of cultivated men is often a survival of this order in various particulars. But, in view of such an order of ideas, shall we say that the primeval man's conception of himself as *having a soul* was a pitiful *mis*conception which has been perpetuated to the present time? Yes his conception of himself as *having a soul*. This *was* a misconception. But this misconception was his puerile explanation of the fact that he *was* a soul: the fact I say, for, if it be not a fact, its not being so yet remains to be shown. In his latest utterance, Professor Tyndall has confessed his inability to make any such showing. What the primeval man could not account for — the mystery of consciousness — no more can he. "We have made no step," he says, "towards its solution." And again, "A mighty mystery still looms, before us, and thus it will ever loom." "It is no "explanation," he continues, "to say that the "subjective and objective are two sides of one "and the same phenomena. Why should phenomena have two sides? There are plenty of molecular motions which do not exhibit this two-sidedness. Does water think or feel when it runs into frost ferns upon a window-pane? If not, why should the molecular motions of the brain be yoked to this mysterious companion consciousness?"

It was to account for "this mysterious companion consciousness" that the primeval man resorted to his crude philosophy of sleep and dreams. It was the analogy of sleep and death which first suggested to him that "this mysterious companion consciousness" was still existent when it came back no more into its former tenement, looked out no more from the poor sightless eyes. But it is not as if this primitive idea of immortality had not been revised a thousand times since its original genesis. At this remove, it is in vain to try to bring discredit on the doctrine by taunting it with the provisional form it first assumed. The deepening of man's self-consciousness insured its continuity. What wonder that uncultivated men distinguished sharply between that mystic *I* and its bodily environment, when even the most searching scrutiny of modern science is totally unable to express consciousness in physical terms! And certainly, till science can do this, the hope of immortality is indefeasible for those who care to cherish it.

But a hope is one thing and a dogma is another. The dogma of immortality, as a Christian dogma, rests, with conscious security, upon the fact, or supposed fact, of the resurrection of Jesus from the dead. It has been the habit of the Christian preacher, in the great majority of instances, to insist upon the absolute futility of all other evidence, the absolute sufficiency of this. To this day there are Unitarian ministers who assure their congregations that if this fails, "The pillared firmament is rottenness and earth's base built on stubble;" that elsewhere there is not a hint of consolation. If this be so, the sooner we abandon every hope of immortality the better. Better expect the worst, and then, perhaps, be gloriously disappointed, than hang our hope upon so fine a thread as Jesus' resurrection. For even if this were an incontestable fact, what would it prove? Says a Unitarian minister, "If the body of Jesus should now be found in some Jewish sepulchre, my faith in immortality would be gone." The meaning is that then he would be sure it did not ascend up into heaven. But how does the ascension of Jesus into heaven, "with his flesh and bones," as the Prayer Book of the Church of England boldly but honestly phrases it, argue our *bodiless* ascent, immediately on the event of death or at some distant resurrection in our rehabilitated flesh? But Jesus was a supernatural being, a god or demigod or super-angelic or angelic being. How then does his resurrection prove any thing for us? What man has done man may do, but not necessarily what some super-human being may do in virtue of his supernatural power. But even if the fact of Jesus' resurrection were a sufficient proof of universal immortality, who shall assure us of the fact. The principal documents relating it, the four gospels, made their appearance from seventy-five to one hundred years after the death of Jesus. The different narratives abound in contradictions which no ingenuity can harmonize. Agreeing in such particulars as are natural and easy to believe, they differ in all others. The nearest approach we make to the event is in Paul's account of it in his Epistle to the Corinthians. He relates the different appearances of the risen Jesus, and winds up his testimony, "And last of all he was seen of me also." So then he did not regard any of the previous appearances as different from that which he had himself enjoyed, which was a manifest hallucination. His vision was unshared by his companions. Such testimony is the ruin of the argument. And yet the resurrection of Jesus has for eighteen centuries been the foundation of the Christian's hope of immortality! Was ever so much believed upon such paltry evidence? Did ever pyramid so huge rest on so frail an apex?

Whatever the resurrection of Jesus might prove, it cannot itself be proved; and, if proved ever so conclusively, it would only prove that Jesus rose again, not that one other ordinary mortal could do that which he accomplished only in virtue of his supernatural power. Equally inefficacious are the teachings of Jesus on this head, however authoritative they are allowed to be. There are many passages in the New Testament which assert the immortality of the believer. There is hardly one which asserts the natural and universal immortality of man. The nearest approach to such an assertion ascribed to Jesus is the merest verbal quibble which, let us hope, he never uttered. The Sadducees denied the resurrection, and Jesus is represented as confounding them with the Old Testament phrase "the God of Abraham and Isaac and Jacob." If he is the God of these, they must be still alive or destined to revive, "for God is not the God of the dead, but the God of the living." This is the sort of argument that was convincing eighteen hundred years ago! But even if Jesus had affirmed the natural and universal immortality of man a hundred times in unmistakable language, his affirmation would not prove any thing but his belief. If we can trust the record, he believed in demoniacal possession, in a personal devil, in a literal, fiery hell. The genius of Jesus was not intellectual, but moral. He accepted the doctrines current in his time, and made them the vehicles of his enthusiasm for righteousness. We are not called on to believe any thing upon his *ipse dixit*. And, if we were, we cannot be certain that he said one single thing that is ascribed to him in the New Testament.

The instinctive or intuitive belief of men in immortality, inside of Christendom, has rested almost entirely on the resurrection of Jesus and the assumption of his authoritative teaching. To the extent that it has done so, the intuition is discharged of all validity. It makes no difference that the modern intuition is not consciously based on these foundations. If a child is not legitimately born, his ignorance of his parentage does not make him any more legitimate. The intuition being thus discredited by the explanation of its genesis and growth, and the direct argument from the resurrection or the teachings of Jesus proving, at the same time, worthless, what other arguments are there to take the place of this? Christian theology has for the most part denied that there are any, in order thus to enhance the reverence of men for its peculiar dogma. But there have always been some Christian theologians who have been pleased to think of Christianity as a republication of natural religion. Such have been glad to fortify their supernatural position with outworks of natural reason. And there have always been still wiser men than these, whom the apparent insufficiency of the supernatural has compelled to seek for other and more satisfactory arguments. Let us consider some of these.

One is that the soul is immaterial, and therefore cannot perish. In such an argument, there is nothing worth considering. Who told you that no immaterial thing can perish? And are you absolutely certain that the soul is immaterial? An astonishing syllogism this, in which the major and the minor premises are equally assumptions pure and simple. If only we were certain that the soul is a material substance, then indeed we might be certain of its indestructibility. But if it is a material substance, as some have ingeniously argued, this substance has so far eluded all investigation.

Another argument for immortality is based on the universality of the belief in it. But the belief in it is not universal, and the only unbelievers are not, as was once assumed, the idiots. Huxley and Tyndall and Morley are several removes from idiocy. And there are hundreds who have nearly as much intellect as these and quite as little faith. And there are other breaks in the chain of universality much more significant than these, involving the absence of this belief, at least in any vital form, from mighty populations. But even if there were not a single break in it, even if the belief were absolutely universal, I do not see that it would prove the fact. Did not men universally believe for thousands of years that the sun went round the earth, while all the time the earth was going round the sun? "Whom God deceives are well deceived," said Goethe; which I interpret that the universal misconceptions of humanity are necessary steps in the evolution of intelligence, and so do not impeach the sanity or integrity of the universal order.

Another argument for immortality closely allied with this from universal belief is that from universal desire.

> "Whatever crazy sorrow saith,
> No life that breathes with human breath
> Has ever truly longed for death.

> "Tis life whereof our nerves are scant,
> O life, not death, for which we pant,
> More life, and fuller, that I want."

It may be so, although the Buddhist longing for Nirvana is a remarkable chapter in the book of universal desire for immortality. But the Buddhist longing for Nirvana, which was as near as might be to annihilation, was no doubt the outcome of intolerable social conditions. Such have often resulted in a passionate desire for immortality. Apparently the conditions of Hindu life were so intolerable that the victim could not conceive of any life that would be worth the having. But even if the desire for immortality were universal, I do not see that this would prove the fact any more than would a universal belief. It is easy enough to say with Fourier, "The attractions are proportioned to the destinies." But every man of us has proved the falsity of this in his own personal experience. The desire for immortality, if universal, might still be only the ideal exponent of the universal instinct of self-preservation, — here rendered more intense by the satisfactions, and there by the disabilities of the present life.

Another argument is from the need of immortality, not the *felt need*, which is equivalent to the desire which we have just considered. Light for the eye because it needs it, air for the lungs because they need it, and so immortality for the soul because it needs it. But in our new philosophy it is the light that builds the eye; the air that builds the lungs. Is it the immortality that builds the soul? Sure of the need of immortality, and it would indeed imply a radical defect in the divine order for there to be no provision for such a need. But if you are going to prove the need of immortality, you must go much deeper than these analogies of light and air.

Men say that it is needed for the reward and punishment of deeds done in the body. But, to my thinking, all such deeds are adequately punished and rewarded here and now. Still there are times when there appears to be no outward retribution, when evil courses do not seem to mar the body's strength; when the dishonest man goes unsuspected, and the honest man is unjustly suspected and condemned. Why but because the reward of every good or evil action is immediate. "Blessed are they who are persecuted for righteousness' sake, for theirs *is* the kingdom of heaven." *Is now*, not will be by and by. So far is this assigned relation between immortality and virtue from being an argument for the former, that it is the greatest evil which it has to answer for. It has demoralized morality. It has prevented men's 'pursuing virtue virtuously.' It has infected goodness with ulterior greed. It is a monstrous thing to say that, if there is no other life, then this can be degraded without blame.

"Hath man no second life? *pitch this one high.*"

The purest sanction and the grandest inspiration of morality is the necessity which is laid upon us by our innumerable benefactors, in the past and present, of doing what we can to make life sane and sweet for those around us and those who will come after us.

Another argument for immortality is the inequality of human conditions. Scriptural sayings are not wanting in support of such an argument, "Go to, ye rich men, weep and howl, for you have received your consolation." "Now Lazarus is comforted, and you, Dives, are tormented." The New Testament idea is that, under the new *régime*, the poor of this world are going to be rich, and *vice versâ*. Hence voluntary poverty with a view to being a celestial millionnaire. This formerly, but latterly voluntary poverty is infrequent. Men prefer being millionnaires now, and risking "the sweet by and by." Is the equality of human fortunes in another life any more desirable than their reversal? Is the inequality here so great as is imagined? I would not change with any living Vanderbilt or Stewart. It may be yonder scavenger would not if he could get inside their inner consciousness. Again, of human inequality how much is the result of strenuous well-doing on the one hand; of neglect upon the other? But there is real inequality for which the victim is not consciously or actually responsible. Yes; but it is no proof of immortality. If the unseen power is such a power that it can permit inequality here, why not elsewhere? It may be the defect of his excellence. It may be, it *is*, an incident of social evolution, a temporary maladjustment, which, so far as need be, the wisdom of the coming generations will correct.

I am aware that a complete survey of the arguments by which the modern mind sustains its faith in immortality ought to include the remarkable development called Spiritualism, which has been so conspicuous within the last five and twenty years. Within the boundaries of Christendom, it can be safely said there is no faith in immortality so strong and glad as that of the Spiritualist. His other life is an extension of the present, with its attendant occupations and delights. While the average Christian faith is conventional, the Spiritualist's is thoughtful. His thought may not be always logical; but it is thought, and not mere acquiescence. He means it shall be scientific. And if he has been treated scornfully by many scientific men, he has converted others,— not a few; among them, Alfred Wallace, the co-discoverer with Darwin of the principle of natural selection, the peer of any scientist now living. Of such a development as this, the epithets of Carlyle, " ultra-materialism, ultra-brutalism," are not exhaustive, whatever elements inhere in it to which these epithets belong.

I do not speak from personal experience, but I believe that Spiritualism has developed certain wonderful phenomena, for which the evidence is a thousand times as strong as for any New Testament wonder. But between these phenomena and the affirmation that they are caused by disembodied spirits, the gulf is one I cannot leap, for it is simply infinite. In the absence of other known causes of phenomena, to predicate spiritual intervention seems to me precisely on a par with the proceedings of the prehistoric man, who posited a ghost as the efficient cause of every thing he could not otherwise explain. Until we have sounded the abyss of man's intelligence, and mapped out all the possible relations of mind with mind, we have no right to predicate an unknown agent. So much is evidently the mere reflection of the seeker's mind upon the medium's, or the discoloration of the medium's own, that the anticipation that all may be one of these things or the other is not irrational. Messages claiming to be from my departed friends have frequently been brought to me. I know they never came from them. They have not the accent of their individuality. If they have fallen so from their original estate, I could desire their death had been complete annihilation. "If these reports are true," says Mr. Emerson, "we must invent a more definite suicide," something that will be equally fatal to mind and body. .I would give as much as any one to really hear from my lost friends, but I must not fool myself into mistaking the echo of my voice, or any go-between's, for their celestial talk.

The Swedenborgian doctrine is the oligarchic, autocratic counterpart of Spiritualism, which is essentially democratic. The Swedenborgians hate the Spiritualists more than they do the sceptics, because they have questioned their monopoly. But there is as good evidence that a thousand spiritualist mediums have been *intromitted* into the spiritual world, as that Swedenborg was so *intromitted*. And so the evidence of the spiritualist revelation is a thousand times as good as that of the Swedenborgian. On the other hand, the ethical wisdom of Swedenborg is much superior to any which Spiritualism has yet developed, to my knowledge. It is here that Swedenborg cannot be too highly praised. But when he talks of heaven, all is so stupid and mechanical that to invent a method of annihilation would be the sole enthusiasm and relief of its unhappy population.

The Spiritualist and Swedenborgian frequently plead the comfort of their views as a ground of their validity. Here is no argument; rather a bribe. If I were sure that comfort is the chief end of man, then it would be an argument. But I am not sure of this; no one is sure of it. Nor do I want a world with so much comfort in it that there is no room for courage, none for simple endurance, since without the opportunity for these humanity would shrivel to a fraction of its present amplitude. That a doctrine is comforting cannot prove that it is true in such a world as this, where the unseen power is not always soft with us, but sometimes stern enough. As with special forms, so with the general doctrine: its truth has been inferred from its comfortable aspect. I find a better argument for it in the fact that men have clung to it in spite of any lack of comfort. For, taken all the way through, not comfort, but lack of comfort, has been its most conspicuous quality. Than the assumption that the doctrine of immortality has always been pre-eminently comforting, nothing could be more unwarranted. Taken through all its course, its terrors have a thousand times outweighed its charms. It is only within the present century that it has assumed that sentimental form which makes it seem so comforting. But to this day, for the deeply thoughtful, it has certain aspects so painful that it sometimes appears to them a doubtful good, and more desirable the lot

"Of happy men that have the power to die."

So far I have had a most ungracious office

laid upon me: to convict one after another of the popular arguments for immortality of insufficiency. It would have been vastly pleasanter to find each one of them sufficient by itself, and all of them together overwhelmingly so. Was never assurance of immortality more strong, was never dream of it more beautiful, than the assurance and the dream I would have built for you out of these popular arguments, if they would have borne their own weight, and lent each other a little mutual support. And it may be that I have undervalued them. The temptation to overvalue them is so strong that, in attempting to resist this, I may have erred upon the other side. But better so than give you doubtful reasons. If we suspect a leak in our ship's hold, let us not walk her sunny deck in feigned security. Let us go down into her hold, and rummage there, and see what is the matter. First, last, and always, let us know the facts. Once known, we can, I am persuaded, adjust ourselves to them in some creditable manner. But to cherish an illusion is to forfeit that self-respect which is the good man's best estate, the fountain of his purest consolation.

Let us know the facts. But there are other facts than those involved in our destructive criticism of the popular intuition and its argumentative supports. First of all, there is this stupendous fact of consciousness, of personality. This I have said already is the indefeasible basis of our hope of immortality. Here it is; and science, in the person of her most "vigorous and rigorous" hierophant, declares that she has made no step towards the solution of its mystery. That this consciousness has somehow emerged from matter, science is confident; but of the manner of this emergence she does not presume to speak. It is as inconceivable in the brain as it would be in a grape-vine or a piece of granite. But here it is; of all things the most indubitable. What a stupendous marvel is here: matter becoming conscious of itself; interpreting the universe, thinking God's thoughts after him! What does it show if not that life and thought were somehow resident in matter from the first? Else how emerged? It is superfluous to say that science cannot predicate the destruction of "this mysterious companion" with the dissolution of the body. That which she cannot express in any physical term, that which she cannot connect with any function of the body or the brain, is absolutely safe from her destroying hand. If she cannot affirm its superiority to the accident of death, no more can she deny it. And in this inability we have the negative condition of a boundless hope for all who wish to cherish it.

To this negative condition let us see what can be added. This positive condition first of all: the persistency in some form of this force of personality. It may be dissipated, but it cannot be destroyed. Whether it is matter or force, this is equally certain. Now then, suppose a Shakspere, tired of the life of the metropolis, having made a snug fortune, which he is pleasantly conscious of, and a fame world-wide and century-enduring, which he is hardly conscious of at all, goes back to Stratford with the hope of living there a quiet, comfortable life, when suddenly some malady swoops down upon him: he dies, and his dust is stored away under the little church in which he meant to be a decent worshipper. Shall we follow the fortunes of the body with the eye of the imagination, hoping to find in any intimation what became of that, in certain gases, certain growths of vegetable and animal life, a sufficient conservation of the energy that could produce the mirth of Falstaff, the tenderness of Cordelia, the fascinating loveliness of Juliet, the graver charm of the much-suffering Desdemona, the doubt of Hamlet, and the awful tragedy of Lear? To think of such a thing is to confute it. But, if the conservation of energy be indeed a law, if it runs all the way through the world of matter and of spirit, the force which constituted Shakspere's soul must somehow be conserved. And for such conservation we cannot be put off with any immortality of fame, or influence, or affection, or social perpetuity. There is nowhere here any sufficient conservation of the energy that was still vital in the poet when disease and death arrived. All this had been provided for, and still the mighty intellect remained. And, in one form or another, it must remain unto this day; else is there no law of the conservation of energy.

But the conservation of energy does not signify its continuous identity. The energy is oftenest conserved by transmutation. The heat becomes motion or the motion heat. To our indefeasible negative ground of hope we have then added only so much of a positive element as is suggestive of the persistency of the force embodied in our consciousness. But if this force should suffer such a transmutation as that of heat into motion, there would be no resumption of our conscious, individual life beyond the grave. Is there, then, any positive element suggestive of the continuous identity and self-consciousness of the individual soul? There is; and it inheres in the perception of the fact that in man, the highest product of natural selection, begins a process of voluntary selection, of conscious self-improvement, and of conscious devotion to the progressive tendency of the universal order. Can you conceive that when the eternal Power has, as the last result of millions of years of patient evolution, fashioned a being, who can echo his own wonderful I AM, who can be a conscious fellow-laborer with him in carrying on the sweep of evolution to still grander heights, he should be so unthrifty as to resolve this being back again into unconsciousness? The words are anthropomorphic, but the thought is not necessarily so. I am reminded of those wonderful words of the apostle, " The earnest expectation of the creation longeth for the manifestation of the sons of God." Good science that! Good evolution! And when this manifestation has at length been consummated, I dare believe that Nature will somehow secure her work, henceforth her conscious workman, against any loss of that which is the crown of her rejoicing. " The mighty energy that is enwrapped " in the human will, the indomitable sense of " duty that tramples down tempting pleasures, "and impels man to conflict and self-sacrifice "for the right, the wealth of love that he lavishes "and that no limit of years exhausts, the un- "satisfied spirit within him, for ever peering "over the barriers of knowledge in search of "new realms of truth: — as these testify to a "past eternity which has been used in producing "them, so do they point forward to a future "eternity, which they are to use as conscious "creative forces in the universe of God."[1]

Another positive element in support and confirmation of our indefeasible hope inheres in the concomitance of such a hope with all that is most beautiful and noble in our intellectual and moral life. For in the natural order of events I hold that nothing is more certain than that the hope of immortality is organized in us more definitely by every higher thought, or nobler act, or purer purpose of our lives. It is not as if we went about deliberately to make our hope more eager, but it is made more eager in the natural order of our lives, just in pro-

[1] Rev. William J. Potter.

portion as we seek great ends, live for the imperishable things of truth and righteousness. Can it be possible that there is such a contradiction at the inmost heart of things, that every higher thought, or nobler act, or purer purpose, tends to immerse us deeper in a terrible illusion? Are not a thousand and ten thousand voices of science blending to assert the solidarity of universal nature and life? Can there be contradiction and confusion only here where life reaches its highest level, or must there be some "pre-established harmony" between our hope and some sublime reality? If the almost invariable concomitant of the noblest living is this glorious hope, then unless Nature is divided against herself, does not this almost invariable concomitance suggest with overwhelming seriousness that the same power which organizes in us the purest splendors of our thought and love organizes in us the hope of an immortal life, in which these splendors shall go on and on from glory to glory. Here is an element so positive in confirmation of our hope that at times it seems to me to have the force of scientific demonstration.

But let us keep clearly within bounds. "No demonstration, but a hope," says Dr. Bartol. It is best so. It must be if God is good, or, as the agnostic might prefer to phrase it, if the universe is sane. If demonstration had been best, then demonstration would have been the order of the day. "No demonstration, but a hope." But once sure of our hope, once sure that it is indefeasible, as we can be negatively from the total inability of science to express our consciousness in physical terms, and positively, because all force is indestructible, because natural selection becomes voluntary in us, and because this hope is the almost invariable concomitant of our highest spiritual life,— once sure of our hope and we can leave it free to be expanded, purified, ennobled by all our various intellectual and moral and affectional life. The more wonderful the realization of this hope appears to us, the more reasonable will it appear at the same time; such being the average make of things, that the more wonderful any thing is, so it be truly wonderful, the more likely is it to be true. We need not go about to nurse the fibre of our hope with wilful energy. We have only to live a rich and full and loving and harmonious life, and every stream from every height will swell this rushing river, and fertilize its banks with tenderer and more fragrant flowers. Reading great books, hearing great music, seeing great pictures, it will seem quite impossible to us that the creators of these things should not outlast their works. But these achieve a sort of immortality, as members of "the choir invisible, whose music is the gladness of the world." Shakspere and Homer are more alive and regnant now than when they were in the body, thanks to their literary monuments. But you and I have known men and women, the latchets of whose sandals Homer and Shakspere were not worthy to unloose: they were so pure and true. They leave behind them neither books nor paintings, but none the less our hope of immortality is nourished at the stainless fount of their immeasurable consecration. We cannot make them dead. We stand beside their silent forms and look upon their faces. How like our friends, and yet how infinitely different! Where is that "mysterious companion" whose absence makes this infinite difference? We cannot say, but standing there, our hope that somehow, somewhere, it survives, a conscious individual life, receives immense acceleration. I say not that at such times I *am* certain of immortality. But what I say is, that at such times I *feel* as certain of it as of my own existence. I have known men and women whose real death was an unthinkable proposition; as much so as a square circle or the meeting of two parallel lines. Might not our own be so to us, if we should live the truest and divinest life we know?

Doubtless to some of you the hope for which I plead will seem a thin and colorless abstraction. But so that you do not forget that you are hoping, not affirming, you can fill out my meagre outline as completely as you choose, and your hope will have the same validity that any imaginative presentation of the other world has ever had. For every such presentation has been without authority. Shall we meet our friends? Shall we know them? Shall we be with them? Religious sentiment has answered all these questions according to our heart's desire. But the answers are without any warrant of the Bible or the creeds. Not a syllable did Jesus lisp concerning any of these things. Only remember that you are hoping, not affirming, and you may hope as bravely as you like; ay, even as I do, that

> "sudden the worst turns the best to the brave;
> The black minute's at end,
> And the elements' rage, and the voices that rave,
> Shall dwindle, shall blend,
> Shall change, shall become first a peace, then a joy,
> Then a light, then thy breast,
> O thou soul of my soul! I shall clasp thee again,
> And with God be the rest!"

And yet I would that all of us might hold our hope of immortality in strict subordination to our faith in the eternal Power who worketh all things well. The ideal attitude is reached when we can say in our Gethsemanes of loneliness and grief, when we have hoped our hope of immortality with the utmost tenderness and passion of our souls, "Nevertheless not as I will, but as Thou wilt." Our relation to the idea of immortality reaches its highest form, its purest possible religiousness, when it arrives at this. This is the supreme self-sacrifice. The depth of our desire measures the height of our self-abnegation. Well may our barks sink, if to this deeper sea! When, hope as you will, you can trust every thing to the Eternal, then does the peace that passes understanding overflow your heart with its ineffable serenity. And can you *not* trust every thing to him when you consider all the ordered beauty and beneficence of his manifest life? Hope then, dear friends, as grandly as you will, but still more grandly trust.

> "We men, who in our morn of youth defied
> The elements, must vanish. Be it so!
> Enough if something from our hands have power
> To live and act and serve the future hour;
> And if, as toward the silent tomb we go,
> Through love, through hope, and faith's transcendent dower,
> *We feel that we are greater than we know.*"

JANUARY 26, 1879.

V.

CONCERNING PRAYER.

WHETHER the function of prayer is an obsolete superstition, or still adequate in one form or another to the demands of scientific truth and rational religion, is a question of such serious and almost painful import that one does not approach it without hesitation and anxiety, lest he should think or speak of it misleadingly. But it is a question which is engrossing so largely the attention of the more thoughtful part of every civilized community, that the teacher of religion is hardly permitted to excuse himself from speaking of it to his habitual congregation in such fashion as he may. Meantime the great majority of religious people, Christian and others, are not afflicted with any doubt or hesitation in regard to this important matter. A perfect confidence in the efficacy of prayer is the prevailing mood; and between objects for which it is admissible to pray and objects for which it is not, the average mind makes no distinction. Material commodities and spiritual benefits jostle each other in the petitions of the devout believer; the former coming in for their full share of urgency, especially if we reckon under this head, as in strict propriety we should, the comforts and felicities of a prospective state of being. And if the ultimate test of any form of creed or conduct is the warrant of antiquity, and particularly of that segment of antiquity which is reported in the Jewish and early Christian scriptures included in the Bible, then it must be confessed that all the argument is on the side not only of prayer, but of prayer in every possible form, for every conceivable object. There is no selfishness or crudity or indelicacy or mechanism or audacity of modern prayer which cannot find some prototype in the most ancient times, in the Bible or out of it, and in the theory and practice of the most conspicuous teachers of religion. The earliest prayers of which we have any knowledge are frank requests for grain and cattle, for a numerous progeny, — now seldom prayed for or desired, — for success in war and rapine, for defence against disease and poverty and death. Oftenest the prayer was a propitiation of a malicious or offended deity, or an attempt to bribe one deity to interfere and thwart the malevolent intentions of another. In Homer and Virgil, the suppliants are on the alert to get the strongest god upon their side. To this end, they coax him and flatter him, appeal to his pride, threaten him, and so on. In the same way, the gods pray to each other. We see Jupiter and his ox-eyed Juno arrayed on different sides, haggling with and plotting against each other. Where, as among the Hebrews, polytheism had a tribal root, there was the same endeavor to engage the help of the most potent deity. And Jacob vowed a vow saying, "If Jehovah will be with me and will keep me in this way that I go, and will give me bread to eat and raiment to put on, then shall Jehovah be my God." The spirit here evinced is that of the free and independent voter determined to cast his vote for that candidate who will pay the most for it. The worshipper is resolved to put his prayer, as the congressman his money, where it will do the most good. We find Moses saying to Jehovah substantially, "Shame on you! what will the gods of the other nations and their retainers think of you, if you do thus and so?" There was once a New England farmer who affirmed that he had prayed in the corner of every lot upon his many-acred farm,—prayed that the Lord would punish his enemies. A great many of the Old Testament prayers are of this sort. The psalms especially abound in them. "Elias prayed earnestly that it might not rain, and it did not rain for the space of three years and six months." The prayer of Elijah brought down fire from heaven to burn wood and to lick up water. In the New Testament it is written, "All things whatsoever ye ask in prayer, believing, ye shall receive." That is very comprehensive. Of course the word "believing" furnishes a convenient loop-hole for the modern pietist to back out of. When the prayer is not answered, we are assured it is because of unbelief. So with James's assertion, "The prayer of faith shall save the sick, and the Lord shall raise him up." Within a few years, there have been legal proceedings against a sect in England called the Peculiar People, who practised this method as a substitute for medical treatment. Again, it is promised in the New Testament, "If two of you shall agree on earth, as touching any thing they shall ask, it shall be done for them by my father who is in heaven." Hence the concentric fire of prayers at stated seasons. Hence the suggestion, a few years ago, that all the churches should pray for the appearance of a fiery cross in heaven on a certain night, in attestation of the truth of certain dogmas of religion. The longer-headed hastened to prevent such an arrangement. But the logic of the situation entirely justified it. Prayer and the dogma being what men claim, the deity would have been in honor bound to make the cruciform display. Once more, we have in the New Testament the parable of the unjust judge, who, though he would not hear the woman because of the justice of her cause, did finally hear her "because of her importunity." Here is the Biblical excuse for the persistent praying of the modern pietist, for the idea that God can be tired out and compelled to give in if the petitioner does not give out.

Said I not truly, then, that if the ultimate test of any form of creed or conduct is the warrant of antiquity, and particularly the warrant of the Bible, there is no boldness or crudity or mechanism or audacity of modern prayer that cannot find this warrant? Let us say it frankly: The man who does not go behind the Bible, who does not feel at liberty to question any statement it contains, to whom it is the final court of appeal, who regards its every verse and chapter as the direct inspiration of the Almighty, — such a man is perfectly consistent in praying for any temporal commodity, for the suspension of any physical law, in arranging such a concentric fire against the stony heart of God as shall break down its walls of adamant, and enable the besieging army to rush in and rifle all the treasure of its love, and drench itself with all the wine of its dear pity. Such a man has not only Bible warrant for these modes of prayer, he has the warrant of the universal Christian tradition. Montalembert, a most learned and pious Roman Catholic, says that prayer is stronger than omnipotence. It can compel God. He cannot resist the entreaties of his saints. There is a remarkable passage in the writings of Martin Luther, in which his prayers and their successful outcome are described in the terms of a tremendous physical encounter, in which, having got uppermost, he, Luther, pummels his antagonist until he cries for mercy, and promises to concede every thing that is asked for. Of late, the air has rung with blasphemies; but no approach has yet been made to this appalling illustration of the invincibility of prayer.

But it will be allowed, at least by all Protestants, that, were the Bible warrant wanting, these later manifestations would not be of much account. The Bible warrant is the stronghold of the popular philosophy of prayer. If we cannot go behind the Bible, if there is no higher court of reason to which we may appeal from its positions, if it is proper to regard it as literally and infallibly the word of God,—then is the popular philosophy of prayer worthy of all acceptance and of the freest application.

But these *ifs* are tremendous. You all know very well that the Bible has a natural history, and that this natural history is such as to bring every doctrine it contains to the bar of reason and discredit it if a verdict of "not true" is rendered there. It is no longer permissible for any intelligent person to engage in any line of conduct or belief simply and only because it has Biblical warrant, seeing that for the most part we are ignorant as to when the different parts of the Bible were written, and by whom they were written. Manifestly, it is a gratuitous stultification of one's self to accord to writings of this description any other authority than they possess in virtue of their intrinsic rationality. For the same reason, we should let no reverence for the personal character of Jesus, or zeal for his infallibility, affect our judgment of beliefs that bear his superscription in the record, seeing that there is not a sentence in the Bible of which we can be absolutely sure that Jesus uttered it. Paint the result of criticism an inch thick with subterfuges, and to this favor it must come.

The question then arises, to be answered upon purely rational grounds, What functions of prayer, if any, are still valid? It is of no use to say that this fruit of prayer is so fine that it disdains the handling of argument, that by such handling all its delicate bloom is worn away and all its beauty marred. The question has been forced upon us by the development of scientific thought. It is of no use to pretend indifference. We cannot feel it. "He that doubteth is damned, *if he eat*."

> "The doubt that saps the life
> Is doubt half-crushed, half-veiled; the lip-assent
> Which finds no echo in the heart of hearts."

But, first of all, I must insist that the validity of prayer is not involved in the validity of the popular conception of the nature of prayer. If it were, there would be no more praying possible for me. For the popular conception of prayer, the average theological conception, involves a miracle in every answered prayer. Prayer thus conceived is the human side of special providence. In every instance of successful prayer, the deity is supposed to interfere with, to suspend, the orderly procedure of the universe. The rational religionist contends that no sufficient evidence has yet been produced of any such suspension, of any such interference. The popular religionist, the conservative theologian, in dealing with this matter, habitually confounds the fact, sometimes indubitable, that prayers are answered with the inference that God interferes to answer them. But that a prayer is answered, or, to speak more strictly, that the thing prayed for comes to pass, is no sufficient evidence that God has suspended the orderly procedure of the universe on our behalf. Let us suppose that there are instances where, if we could be certain that the thing which comes to pass would not have come to pass but for our prayer, to infer divine interference would be inevitable. Such instances are prayers involving a wide circle of phenomena, as, for example, prayers for rain, or for abundant harvests, or for immunity from storms at sea, or for the cessation of a pestilence. To be certain in such instances that prayer was answered — that is, that it had produced the desired effect — would, let us suppose, be equivalent to a certainty that God had interposed to bring about the state of things desired. For though in some of these instances a certain reflex influence of prayer is possible, as in the matter of the harvest or the pestilence, it could not be to any great extent. The conditions of the problem would remain comparatively undisturbed. In the case of rain or storms at sea, the possibility of reflex action is eliminated altogether. Here, then, absolute certainty that but for the prayer the thing desired would not have come to pass, would be, let us suppose, absolute certainty that God had interposed to answer it. But absolute certainty in a matter of this sort is something that can never be attained. Suppose it should not rain from now till next September, and that then one great concentric prayer for rain, rain, should go up from millions of parched lips, storming the ear of heaven with wildly passionate entreaty, and even while the prayers were straining up, the blessed moisture should begin to fall upon the thirsty fields and the imploring hands of agonized devotion. If the rain came because of the prayer, we would allow that God had interposed to answer it. We would waive all consideration of "the chemico-vital forces set loose by an earnest prayer." We would give God the glory. But how could we feel absolutely certain, even in such a case, that the blessing came in answer to the prayer; that it might not have come if there had been no prayer at all? And if we could not feel certain in such a case, what certainty is possible, when no instance is on record a thousandth part so crucial in its character as this? And so with every similar experiment. How be sure that the storm would have engulfed our loved ones but for our prayer, that "the iceberg moving slowly down into the path of traffic" would not have kept "her fatal appointment with the ship" if we had prayed more ardently, that the crop is bountiful or that the pestilence is stayed because of our entreaty? Because we can never be sure of these things, because there may be coincidence instead of cause and effect, we can never be sure of an interfering deity or in other words (those of Professor Tyndall) of "a disturbance of natural law quite as serious as the stoppage of an eclipse, or the rolling of the St. Lawrence *up* the falls of Niagara."

The great majority of "answers to prayer" are of such a character that even if we allow their claim, — that the thing obtained would not have been but for the prayer, — it does not follow that there has been any suspension of the orderly procedure of the universe. We must not forget that the imagination is a potent factor in the human organism, and that the attitude of expectant attention has immense subjective influence. We are hardly permitted to doubt that "king's-evil," or scrofula, was really affected by the king's touch, or that the bones of the saints have made rheumatic limbs more pliable. But was the virtue in the objective touch or relic, or in the subjective imagination. A German *savant* discovered the long-venerated bones of a saint to be those of a donkey, but on this account they had not been a whit less remedial. "Any state of the body earnestly expected," says a learned physiologist, "is very likely to ensue." There is a man in Belgium whose hands and feet bleed every Friday, as it were from nails driven into them. The priests say it is a miracle like unto the famous stigmata of St. Francis of Assisi. A commission of medical men, appointed by the government, say it is the result of morbid expectation, the whole energy of the victim's nature being directed to this end, so flattering to his ecclesiastical pretensions. But this principle of expectant attention is not now responsible for as many answers to prayer as formerly. There are, however, two celebrated institutions in Germany where patients are treated for various mental and some bodily diseases by prayer, and it is said the cures are many. But as the patients are also treated by fresh air and out-of-door life and pleasant scenery, and have much quiet and no medicine, it may be that the prayers are not the secret of recovery. "It is beyond all question or dispute," said Voltaire, "that magic words and ceremonies are quite capable of destroying a whole flock of sheep, if the words be accompanied by a sufficient quantity of arsenic."

How many prayers are answered, too, because men *over*-hear them, not because God hears them. At any rate the *over*-hearing is sufficient to account for the result. George Müller's famous charity in England is, according to his representations, which may be perfectly sincere, supported entirely by prayer. But by such an avowal, on his part, people who believe in prayer are put upon their honor not to let the institution languish. It is prayer that is at stake, not merely the institution. If Müller had kept his method a profound secret, his receipts might not have been so large, but the test of prayer-alone would have been more effectual. There is a consumptives' home in Boston supported entirely by prayer. It has its contribution boxes in scores of public places, conspicuously labelled with the name *and policy* of the institution. When a people are wasted with famine, it is not even necessary to *over*-hear their prayers for succor. It is sufficient for those who can help them to hear of the fact. This is a quite sufficient prayer *to them*, which they will answer speedily with ship-loads of food seasoned with the tears of a divine compassion. So, too, the need of cities wrapped in flames, or scourged by pestilence, need not be telegraphed to us by way of heaven. It can come direct. The *god in us* hears the afflicting story, and responds to it with needful sustenance. Oh, there is many a prayer that now goes all unanswered that would be answered speedily if but some man or woman could overhear it! But so many prayers are overheard that this element must never be omitted from the problem, Whether the orderly procedure of the universe is ever temporarily suspended in response to our entreaties.

Volumes have been written, full of instances which are supposed to favor the affirmative solution of this problem, not one of which is verifiable, but no volume has so far been written, by the advocates of heavenly interference or by anybody else, enumerating the instances in which the prayer has never had the faintest semblance of an answer. The million volumes in the National Library at Paris would not be sufficient to contain such an enumeration. But is it fair that every instance favorable to the doctrine of interference should be counted and every other instance go for naught? I know the posterns by which men escape from this dilemma. They say that the unanswered prayers were not ardent enough, or persistent enough, or something of that sort. But any one must be stone-blind not to perceive that here we have an arbitrary excuse for a foregone conclusion.

I must confess that there is something horrible to me in men's assurance that God has interfered to save *their* lives, *their* property, *their* friends, but has not interfered to save the lives, the property, the friends of other people. It was a special providence that *they* did not sail upon the missing steamer. What was it, then, for all who did sail, and came back no more? Might God have interfered to save that freight of precious lives, and did not, perhaps because the requisite amount of prayers was not forthcoming. No, no! God does not interfere: the comfortable, the blessed thought is that he cannot interfere. He cannot or he would. I stake my faith in him on this assertion. He suffers no restraint but that of his own infinite perfection. But, thanks to this, one shattered train, one sinking wreck offsets all the imaginary interferences that have ever been recorded, and remands them at once and for ever to the province of coincidence or overhearing or exaggeration. Of what avail the baby-house suggestion, that God, anticipating human prayer, left certain openings in the network of his laws through which he can reach out handfuls of benefits and immunities, — winds out of some Æolian cave, or showers of needed rain, and quiet of the sea or of the heart? Law is an armor so compact that there is not a joint which any interfering touch can penetrate. In the material universe, there is not a space as big as a pin-head for an interfering god to stand upon. The ground is everywhere preoccupied by those persistent habits of the deity which we call laws, — habits which are not a second nature, as we say of ours, but his first and only nature, his essential quality. To pray for so much interference as would quell one coming storm, or squeeze one rain-drop out of a reluctant cloud, is to pray that the entire history of the universe up to date may be revised, and that God may change the essence of his nature with a view to our imaginary comfort or advantage.

There are those who say, in answer to all this, that the so-called laws of nature are only our subjective formulas; that is to say only our classification of such facts as have already come within our ken. It does not follow that there are not other facts. No, it does not. But never was any attempt to find a foot-hold for the supernatural more unfortunate than this. If the laws of nature were not subjective classifications of the observed facts of nature, if they were so many unalterable formulas known to be inclusive of all natural facts, then any fact that did not come within their scope would at once declare itself supernatural. But what makes a miracle impossible, in the sense of a supernatural event, is that the laws of nature, as we call them, *are* subjective classifications of the observed facts of nature; and the moment we come upon a fact not included in them, we are simply obliged to modify our hitherto unduly narrow conception of the laws of nature, so that they will include the latest fact. "The day-fly," says Professor Huxley, "has better grounds for calling a thunder-storm supernatural, than has man, with his experience of an infinitesimal fraction of duration, to say that the most astonishing event that can be imagined is beyond the scope of natural causes." And thus the subjective character of the so-called laws of nature, so far from being a back-door through which the supernatural may find its way into "the house of life," is a mountain-wall which it can never pass. Whatever happens, no matter how wonderful, no matter how unexampled, can only serve to broaden our subjective generalization of law. It cannot possibly transcend it.

And hence it follows that we have been too ready to allow or to suppose that, if it could be proved that but for the prayer A the event B would not have happened, we should have a genuine case of interference. Prove that but for the prayer the drought would not have ceased, and what follows? That there has been an interference of the deity? Certainly not;

but only that our formulas of natural law must be extended so as to include prayer, henceforth, among the data of meteorology, an additional element of uncertainty in all our weather calculations.

Things being as they are, it is impossible to predicate an interfering deity at any point in the illimitable sweep of prayer, from the early Aryan's frank petition "that we may prosper in getting and keeping" to the most spiritual prayer a Robertson or Channing ever breathed. There are many people who do not demur at this result, so long as it is understood to cover only the material side of prayer, — petition for objective benefits, health, wealth, and safety, and so on, — who, nevertheless, are hurt and troubled, when it is proposed to extend the application to prayer for spiritual benefits, — for peace of mind, for strength of will, for purity of heart. Men pray for purer purposes, for better dispositions, for broader charity, for faithfulness to their ideals of truth and righteousness. That it must be ennobling and exalting to proffer such petitions no one is likely to deny. If we fall to work and help the deity to answer our petitions, the benefit accruing may be beyond all estimate. But if, refusing to deceive ourselves, we put the question squarely, Does God interfere to answer these petitions any more than those for health, or rain, or victory in battle? we are obliged to answer, He does not. For, in the first place, that reflex action which in prayers for material blessings is sometimes a very doubtful factor, is here an obvious and very potent energy. Such prayers avail not for ourselves alone, but for our friends. I have heard such, and as I listened to their words of tender pleading, all that was worst in me seemed suddenly to lose its power, all that was best to assert a calm superiority. How could I ever sin against those beautiful ideals of truth and holiness which in that moment I had seen! And I have gone for days in the strength of some such momentary revelation. But there was no need to assume any heavenly interference to account for my access of strength and peace. Is there ever any such need? If roughly, still is it not truly, said, "You will get a virtue no sooner than a salad for the asking." And if, just for the asking, or for any amount of asking, God does not *make us* more charitable or just or honest or sincere or pure or kind, ought we to keep on asking him to make us this or that, whatever incidental benefit accrues? We must not be liars in our devotions. We must not make a show of asking God for this or that, in order that we may economize some reflex influence of our petition.

No miracle, no prayer, insists the popular religionist. But it is just as impossible to prove a miracle in the sense of a suspension of the ordinary course of nature on the spiritual as on the material plane. Prove that the spiritual blessing would not have come without the prayer, and you have proved a relation of co-existence or sequence, of cause and effect; but you have proved no interference. It never can be proved. Establish any fact, and immediately Nature adopts it into her universal order,

> "And gives to it an equal date
> With Andes or with Ararat."

How then? Seeing that no supernatural interference ever has been or ever can be proved, on the material or on the spiritual plane, shall we deny *in toto* the legitimacy of any and of every prayer? Yes, if we accept the would-be axiom of popular religion,—No miracle, no prayer. No, if we do not accept this would-be axiom. And we do not accept it. We deny all miracle, all interference, and at the same time we affirm the legitimacy and dignity and glory and sufficiency of prayer.

But then we do this because we do not define prayer by the inferior limit. If you insist that prayer shall be defined by the inferior limit, that it shall be begging for favors or immunities or miraculous benefits and nothing else, then, verily, for you there is no legitimate, no rational prayer. But, taken all the ages down, prayer has a million times been something over and above all this. Thousands of prayers which have contained this element of selfishness, this beggar cry, this plea for miracle, have contained something else, and something very different. Those of you who have ever studied the development of prayer from the standpoint of evolution know that our modern prayer is the lineal descendant of ancient sacrifice. Hosea, the prophet, indicates the point of transition, when he calls the spoken praise of God "the calves (that is, the sacrificial calves) of the lips." The psalms of the Old Testament represent prayer in its first remove from sacrifice. And they are not so much an asking as a giving. So with the sacrifices that preceded them and kept them company. There were thank-offerings as well as peace-offerings among them. Go back still further, back to the genesis of prayer, to its pre-natal condition. The earliest form of prayer (or rather of its anticipatory phenomena) was the offering of food to the ancestral ghosts. "Come to your home!" chaunted the mourners. "It is swept for you and clean; and we are there who loved you ever. And there is rice put for you and water; come home, come home, come to us again!" In this pre-natal germ of prayer, there is a hint of its sublimest possibility. There is a rebuke of those who insist that if it is not beggary it is nothing. In this pre-natal germ, it was no asking, but a giving. And it is still no asking, but a giving, at its highest point of evolution; a giving certainly, and if an asking, such an asking as implies no interference of the deity with the orderly procedure of the universe.

Prayer is a gift of man to the Eternal. A gift of awe and wonder, reverence, adoration. This is a gift which is appropriate at all times and in all places where it is natural and spontaneous. "That perfect disenthralment which is God" eludes the trap deliberately set for it, but through "the soul's east window of divine surprise" flies in without an invitation.

> "No man can think, nor in himself perceive,
> Sometimes at waking, in the street sometimes,
> Or on the hill-side, always unforewarned,
> A grace of being finer than himself
> That beckons and is gone, a larger life
> Upon his own impinging,"—

no man can have such an experience as this, — and soon or late it comes to each and all, — without bringing his gift to the altar; without that thrill of awe, of reverence, of adoration, which is more truly prayer than thousands of petitions which are proffered in the conventional postures of devotion. And I would have you note, that science, which is the inveterate negation of all prayer that looks for heavenly interference, is to the prayer of adoration a freshet that inundates all its banks with new occasions for its joy. With Lockyer and Darwin and Lyell, we cannot think God's thoughts after him, and not rejoice in the eternal order, as men never could in some imaginary rent in its resplendent folds. The prayer which looks for interference in the eternal order is an imputation of defect. What is this wonderful universe which we inhabit but, as it were, a mighty symphony, into whose melodies and harmonies the Infinite Being has put his whole self, all there is of him; every part, every atom, every law is drenched with deity, — so full of him that not another particle can be obtruded? The prayer that looks for interference is a prayer for more of God. A universe brimful of him is not enough. Dissipate this pitiful illusion, and every particle that is lost upon the side of interference is saved upon the side of that exquisite rapture which "accepts the universe" as an unspeakable good. No longer seeking for benefits or immunities from beyond the circle of the immutable law, it finds this law itself instinct with deity,—better than any possible immunity, of all benefits the best. To see, to accept, to glory in the method and result of universal law,—this is the gift of man's adoring heart to the Eternal. When prayer arrives at such an altitude as this, its words are generally few. When prayer is at its best, it cannot find a voice.

> "I also am a child, and I
>   Am ignorant and weak;
> I look upon the starry sky,
>   And then I must not speak.
> For all behind the starry sky,
>   Behind the world so broad,
> Behind men's hearts and souls doth lie
>   The Infinite of God."

There is a power not ourselves which makes for order and beauty, as well as a power not ourselves that makes for righteousness. The hearts of those old Hebrew men thrilled at the touch of both. What men's have not in any age or land since man emerged from his primeval brutishness! There is no danger that the prayer of adoration will ever flicker and go out upon the altar of devotion. The world might be just as wonderful, just as beautiful as it is, and, if man's mind were different, it might stir in him no sense of mystery, it might awaken in him no delight, no transport of enthusiasm, no rapture of thanksgiving. But so long as the world and humanity remain as they are, made for each other, the mind of man, the natural and genetic complement of the material universe, so long will there be that response of the human spirit to the divine which is of the finest essence of prayer. Certainly, the depth and earnestness of the response is largely proportioned to our thoughtfulness; but, in a universe that is full of visions and of voices, few can so blind or deafen themselves as not to catch some beauty of the one, some music of the other. When the spring comes, as it will so soon, working its blessed transformation, when all the stars in heaven seem out together, when the moon is so white and large that all the stars are dim, when children are born into your homes, when the ineffable mysteries of thought and love entrance your mind and heart, at all such times, and at other times innumerable, we pray as naturally as we breathe. Our prayer is no task-work, but the spontaneous, irrepressible, Godward movement of our hearts, their tidal swell obedient to an infinite attractive power.

Should anybody ask me what is the use of praying in this way, I might find it very difficult to answer them. But that would not be my fault so much as theirs. If a man asks me why he should enjoy the vision of the mountains or the sea, how *can* I answer him? or if he asks me what is the use of enjoying these things? As with the parts, so also with the whole. In one sense, there is no use of feeling that rapture in the presence of the All which is the essence of our adoration. Nobody is any richer for it in gold or land. It pays no dividends. Only the man who kindles with this rapture is infinitely more of a man than one who does not. And what is the use of ever putting this rapture into words, of expressing it, or trying to express it, though we never can, in hymns and spoken prayers? This also pays no dividends. But then no more does lovers' happy talk. It is just telling, each the other, over and over again, that which is known already. It is no use, and yet those who, grown to manhood and womanhood, have not done something in this line at one time or another are greatly to be pitied. "I am a man," said Terence, "and nothing human is indifferent to me." In the best sense of the word, that is the most useful which helps me to be most a man, to bring my experience level with my highest possibility of quickened and multiplied consciousness of life's various good.

And in this sense the glow of adoration, and the poor stammering words in which it tries to body itself forth in hymn or prayer, are second to no other thing in point of use.

To the function of adoration let us add the function of thanksgiving. If this could live upon no other food than the sense of a peculiar and exclusive care for us by the Omnipotent Power, then it might well hunger so for lack of meat as to exhale into the merest ghost of a dead dogma.

"Yes, for me, for me He careth,"

we may still sing, but not as imagining that he is any respecter of persons, that he has any chosen people, any favored child, in all his spacious world. What we are thankful for is, that we are sharers of the universal joy and sorrow of the world. What we are thankful for is, that for all our sorrow and our burden others may be glad and free. The thankfulness of rational prayer does not inhere in any particular blessings, but in the general make and the great sweep of things, the laws so stern and so inflexible, obedience to which can bring to us such peace and joy. When we think of the beauty of the world, of the work we have to do, of our friendships and our homes, of our thought and the great thinkers who assist it, and of the yearnings and the satisfactions of the moral life, and then of how this little life of ours is only one of many millions which the great central life upholds and cherishes, though we may not "pray regular," any oftener than poor Job Leigh in "Mary Barton," yet we shall catch ourselves like him speaking a word with God, and thanking him at odd hours, simply because we cannot help it, any more than Job could when he had had "a fine day for an out." But words are not the only means of self-expression. Murder will out, and so will thankfulness. Sometimes it makes us literally leap for joy. Sometimes its omen is a sudden rush of tears. Sometimes it makes our wives and children wonder what has happened to us that we are so unusually considerate and kind. Sometimes it overflows in little acts of kindness to people we have never seen before and may never see again. To bow the head, to bend the knees, is not a necessary sign of thankfulness. "His port is erect, his face towards heaven," is a more apt description of the man whose heart is full of gratitude to God. No importunity, no prayer? There is a tribe of South Americans who know better than this. They believe their gods are so beneficent that they need ask them for nothing. Nevertheless, they try to express their gratitude to them by simple offerings. As we are of their simple faith, shall we not make their simple habit also ours?

Another function of this rational, non-miraculous prayer, which we are endeavoring to understand aright, is aspiration; which is not *asking* to be made better by any stroke of heavenly interference, but striving to make ourselves better by the slow and patient culture of our every gift. It is the worship of ideal excellence. It declares itself in every effort to secure a body free from weakness or defect, ruddy with health, alive in every sense to its appropriate impressions; in every effort to enlarge the mind with fuller measures of the truth; in every practical resolve to make the reign of conscience more intelligent, and our obedience to its mandates more complete. I would not underrate the value of the faintest impulse in the direction of a purer or a better life. But the aspiration which is equivalent to the highest possible capacity of rational prayer must not be confounded with any such impulse, with any momentary *wish* that we might live more nearly level with our highest possible attainment. Welcome the mountain height or forest depth, the face of man or woman, the poet's thought or mystery of science, that for one moment gives to our horizon infinite expansion! But there is a function of prayer which is more than any thrill of gladness, any rapture of thanksgiving, any momentary impulse of the heart towards what is purest, truest, best. And what is more, unless the worship that is all of these goes forth to seek embodiment in voluntary act, in habitual life, it cannot be expected often to return and animate our dust. Gladness and thanks and trust and adoration are not for idlers, but for men who work. And so the definition of worship as "divine service," familiar to you all, disappears upon one side only to reappear upon the other. The singing of hymns, the reading of a liturgy, the burning of incense, the making of genuflections, the wearing of one ecclesiastical over-garment rather than another, — there is no divine service in all this, no service of God, unless there is some help for man. Prayer is a life, says Zoroaster; a persistent habit of the soul. And we must not be satisfied with any lower definition. Our aspiration must not be fitful and inconstant, here and there in some better moment a feeble wish, a make-believe resolve, so flattering to our moral consciousness. Such aspiration is of small account.

But when aspiration is a constant and unwearied habit of the soul; when year in and year out, we seek for the harmonious perfection of our bodies, minds, and hearts, — then doth the Eternal give to his beloved while they sleep: below the deep of consciousness streams into us the divine power. You have heard of the Thibetan praying-machine, a cylinder on which a famous prayer is pasted, kept revolving in a stream of running water. Hardly less mechanical, I think, are some of the devices of the modern Christian pietist. "Pray for these thirty-five," said the evangelist to a subordinate, on the morning of my visit to his meeting, and Dr. Deems informs us that one day he prays for all his friends whose names begin with A; the next day for all whose names begin with B; and so on through the alphabet. But the Thibetan praying-machine suggests not only the false mechanism of our Christian praying, but also the highest possibility of the most rational prayer that can be offered, for this is realized when the wonderful mechanism of this total life of ours, set in the rushing stream of time and circumstance, the awful current of events, revolving there with marvellous rapidity, becomes itself a prayer inclusive of all others that are worth the making. "The spirit of the living creature is in the midst of the wheels." A prayer is written upon every tissue of the body, upon every fibre of the brain, upon every drop of red arterial blood, upon every thought and feeling and desire; and the answer of this prayer of prayers is the response of the total sanity of the universe to the sanity of our total organism. "Continuing instant in prayer," this is what every true man of us is doing. "Pray without ceasing," this is an injunction which a sound mind in a sound body must perforce obey. Truly there is a God who answers such a prayer as this persistent aspiration, this claim upon the universe of our continuous and total life. But his answer comes to us along no path of interference, but along the grooves of the eternal laws, and so comes very quickly. In town and field, he waits for us in every atom and event, and with rarer gifts than we could ask for, or could even think, responds to our fidelity.

I know that there are some of you to whom the most of what I have said thus far, appears quite reasonable and true; but you conceive there is some incongruity between a theory of prayer so transcendental as this of mine, and almost any possible *form* of public or of private prayer. And certainly I have no disposition to deny that between such prayer as I have been trying to indicate and the majority of spoken prayers, public or private, there is a decided incongruity. I will go further, and will say that there is an incongruity between such prayer and every possible form. But then it is the incongruity which always has existed, and always will exist, between the spirit and the letter, the actual and the ideal. It is the incongruity which exists between the artist's conception and his work. Think you that Michael Angelo ever embodied to the full, in any painting or sculpture, the vision to which he was not disobedient? But how much poorer the world of art would be if he had withheld his hand entirely because he could not, and knew he could not, embody his conception to the full! And how much poorer the world of religion would be if men had never tried to embody in the forms of worship their ideal religiousness! Sometimes, no doubt, the words of prayer shame the reality. But when prayer is at its best, then any words that we can utter, or that the genius of prayer has ever framed, seem all inadequate. The reality of prayer does not necessitate the regularity of private speech with God. I must confess that for myself such regularity of speech or silence is barren of all good. But I do not infer that it is so with all. Let each be his own judge. If the regularity always, or in the majority of instances, brings with it the appropriate emotion, then for you such regularity is best. But others may be no less prayerful whose prayers are spoken, not at noon or eve, but whenever the strong impulse comes upon them. The words are not the prayer. The fewer these, I sometimes think, the better. The saying is that when a god would ride, any thing serves him for a chariot. So when a genuine prayer of adoration, gratitude, and trust would speed to heaven, a single word may bear it up and on.

> "Feeling is all in all; words are but sound and smoke,
> Veiling the glow of heaven."

Happy the man who is so sure of this that he can often make his childhood's earliest prayer the vehicle of his maturest aspiration! Happier if the old words bring back to him his mother's face, his mother's arms, so that, world-worn and weary, for a moment he may know how sweet it is,

> "To lie within the light of God, like a babe upon the breast,
> Where the wicked cease from troubling, and the weary are at rest."

But some of you to whom it seems legitimate for private prayer to clothe itself in words, at regular or irregular intervals, consider public prayer a very doubtful matter. The individual in the secrecy of his chamber and his heart need not be choice of words. He may determine once for all that they are all symbolical;

that they are not scientific, but poetical. And after that, if they do not agree with his rationalized philosophy of prayer, no one is deceived.

> He does not pray because he would;
> He prays because he must,
> There is no meaning in his prayer,
> But thankfulness and trust.

But it is different, men say, with public prayer. Yes, it *is* different. The public prayer is *overheard*, and so the symbol must be chosen with much greater care. But it can hardly be chosen so carefully but that it will still be a symbol, not an exact expression; and therefore the first necessity of all public prayer is that the congregation understand that it is a symbol, not an exact expression. Its language is not scientific, but poetic. Let this be understood, and henceforth all criticism of particular words and phrases is beside the mark; though certainly the congregation have good reason to expect that there shall be some general conformity between the language of devotion and their minister's avowed philosophy.

Once rightly understood, it seems to me that public prayer is wholly natural and beautiful in its idea, whatever it may be in actual experience. Sometimes it is no doubt

> "That drony vacuum of compulsory prayer,
> Still pumping phrases for the ineffable,
> Though all the valves of memory gasp and wheeze."

But Theodore Parker said that never did he stand before his congregation in the attitude of prayer, however dull of heart he had been just before, but that suddenly he felt all the joys and sorrows of his people surging up through his heart and clamoring for expression at his lips. I doubt if those most sceptical of public prayer would not have made an exception in favor of those idyls of devotion. But then they were exceptional. The "drony vacuum" is the rule. Yes, but sometimes the channel, so often muddy when it is not wholly dry, receives such glorious access from all the heights of a man's nature, from all the hidden springs of his experience, that it is not deep enough or wide enough to hold the generous flood. Its banks are broken down and growths of character and endurance that were perishing of drought in other men feel a refreshing coolness at their roots, and throughout every part the promise and the potency of new and better life.

It was said of Edward Everett that his prayers were the most eloquent ever addressed to a Boston audience. But if they were addressed, not to the taste or fancy of his people, but to their conscience, to their justice, truth, and love, the sarcasm is not so very biting. Let us acknowledge frankly that, from one point of view, the public prayer is addressed to the assembled congregation. But none the less is it addressed to God. For it is not as if God were in some "hallowed part" of the wide universe. It is not as if he were not in you and me. And as it is God who is addressed, so is it God who addresses. "As if God did beseech you," said St. Paul. Dr. Hedge writes me, there is but one party in prayer; namely, God. This lofty mysticism is made good most obviously in public prayer, when what is best in me appeals to what is best in you. But is it not equally made good whenever we "summon the good in the depths of ourselves"? Nay in a world where God is all in all, must not all prayer be a divine soliloquy, the sacred converse of the Infinite Being with himself?

The objection to public prayer that it is prayer *for others* is well taken *when it is this*. To pray *for others:* this I must confess, until prayer passes over into action, seems to me quite impossible. But to pray *with* others, having first identified one's self with them, this is legitimate enough. Father Taylor was not much of a philosopher, but his rationale of public prayer was simply perfect when he said, "O God, we are a widow with six children!" So, always, when the preacher truly prays, he is his congregation, the mouth-piece of their gladness and their sorrow, of their peace and pain. As much sympathy, so much true public prayer; no more. Given the sympathy, and it is no longer I that speak, but your spirit that speaketh in me. Then I am yonder mother, busy and anxious with her household cares. Then I am yonder father, troubled, like Martha, about many things, and finding it so hard to keep from being fretful and impatient. Then I am yonder young man, or yonder "happiest girl in the world," so busy with her thoughts of this and that, that she has not the least idea what I say; then I am those among you who are aging, and whose "finest hope is finest memory" projected into dim futurity. Then I am the sorrowing and bereft among you who are trying to take sides with God against yourselves, because you are so sure that your afflictions are but the shadows of his perfectness. Then I am those among you who are seeking that forgiveness for wrong-doing which is inherent in the recuperative forces of the universe. This is the feeling although, it does not always find its way into the fittest words. And sometimes when the feeling is strongest, the words will somehow altogether fail, and the minister will take the Lord's Prayer,[1] or a moment's

---

[1] The best of all *symbols*, because it is composed of
"Words that have drunk transcendent meaning up
From the best passion of all by-gone times."

silence, and put all his feeling into that, at the risk, perhaps, of having others think he is not in a prayerful mood, when he was never in a deeper.

But let us not take leave of one another in this outer court of our great theme. Let us return again, just for a moment, into its inner shrine, its holy of holies, where never any breath of aspiration, thankfulness, or trust, breaks up the silence, or stirs the veil which hangs before the secret place of the Most High; where every wish and hope and aspiration is resolved into a voiceless peace, a trust ineffable.

> "Ask and receive: 'tis sweetly said,
> But what to ask for know I not,
> For wish is worsted, hope o'ersped,
> And aye to thanks returns my thought.
> If I would pray, I've nought to say
> But this, that God may be God still.
> For him to live is still to give,
> And sweeter than my wish his will."

FEBRUARY 9, 1879.

VI.

CONCERNING MORALS.

THE subject of my discourse was never more appropriate than at this moment, when so recently the soil of Massachusetts has been made more sacred than ever by receiving to itself all that could die of one who was, to a degree unparalleled in his day and generation, an incarnation of the Moral Sentiment. Breathing the name of Garrison, we pledge ourselves to the utmost seriousness of thought and speech. It was said of him in 1835 that he had "no visible auxiliary but a negro boy." But he had an invisible auxiliary, — the moral nature of man. Of that invisible auxiliary I am to speak to you this morning.[1]

[1] These introductory sentences, though not a part of this discourse when it was first delivered, are retained, because the name of Garrison is of itself a moral inspiration. They were affixed when the discourse was read before the Free Religious Association, a few days after Mr. Garrison's death.

Wherever human nature is, there is the Moral Sentiment. Can we as certainly affirm, Wherever human nature *has* been, there *has* been the Moral Sentiment also? I should say Yes, on any theory of human origins. Assuming man to be developed from some lower organism, the dawning of the Moral Sentiment would seem to be essential to the idea of human nature. Until this has arrived, the prospective man is something less than human. This is the fairy prince who wakes the sleeping beauty with the kiss so long delayed. If any choose to draw the line which separates humanity from the lower species below this point, they are at liberty to do so. The fact remains, that, wherever we now come in contact with beings whom we agree to call human, there is the Moral Sentiment, there are the antithetic poles of right and wrong, there are the voices saying, *Thou shalt*, and *Thou shalt not;* there are the words and attitudes of praise and blame. In different communities there is a difference in the objects which are regarded as praiseworthy or blameworthy. The savage and barbarian feel morally obliged to engage in certain actions that would be morally impossible for the civilized man, but everywhere appear the opposite poles, the antithetic ideas of right and wrong. This is the most salient feature of the life of man. Eliminate this feature, and you destroy the identity of human nature and of human history, They become something radically different. It is the part of Hamlet in the play, the theme which underlies the symphony, the Niobe who unifies the group, the voice of the chief singer in the choir. Modern critics and devotees of beauty are not wanting who insist that art must never moralize, and that it is wholly independent of morality. And, no doubt, there has been great art devoid of any moral purpose, art that has contented itself with reproducing the beauty of the human face and form, or the beauty of external nature. But the highest form of art is tragedy, epical or dramatic; and the supreme tragedy is the good man suffering calamity. Eliminate the moral element from literature, and you rob Homer and Sophocles, Dante and Shakspere and Goethe, of the most fruitful subject-matter of their art.

Listening to the average pulpiteer, the average moralist, you would suppose that the nature of morality was just as patent as the fact, and that the moral law was "the same yesterday, to-day, and forever;" that conscience always and everywhere dictated one and the same thing. But, in fact, there has been much conflict not only between men unequally developed, but between equally good men, as to what is right and what is wrong; and there has been still more conflict in regard to the essential nature of these opposing facts. But never since the moral life of men began have thought and discussion been so active as they are to-day, concerning the essential nature of morality, its origin, its ground, its sanctions, and so on. This activity results in a considerable degree from the break-down of supernatural religion, but in a more considerable degree from the aggressive energy of the evolutionary theory of human nature. Once let this theory prevail, urge its opponents, and there must be a ruinous catastrophe in the moral order of society. Ay, more: they say that this would already be upon us were not the Darwins and Spencers and Huxleys men of the most lofty personal character. And we are given to understand that it is very mean of them to be so honorable and just. They have no right to be, consistently with their philosophy. But so long as they are so, either from force of habit, or to spite Mr. Mallock and his set, it will be much harder for them to excite the apprehensions of the community than it would be if the evolutionists were a pack of thieves, adulterers, and murderers.

Somehow, — and in the discussion of the moral problem this is a crucial fact, — individual morality is not exclusively dependent on the individual's theory of moral origins or sanctions. It is still possible for a man to live a moral life whether he is an intuitionalist or a utilitarian, a believer in necessity or in the freedom of the will, an advocate of the evolution or of the special creation of the human species. Mr. Mallock insists that Professor Tyndall ought to have a dirty mind; but what is true so far is, that he has such a mind himself, while Professor Tyndall gives no sign, as yet, of following his example. But Professor Tyndall has other opponents whose wit is just as keen as Mr. Mallock's, without being as salacious. Best of all, it is quite as possible for a man to live a moral life without any general theory of morality, as to have his blood circulate in the most perfect manner without knowing any thing about Harvey's theory of its circulation, or any other. Of some of the best men who have lived it may be doubted whether they had a special theory of morals any more than Homer had a theory of the epic poem, or Shakspere a theory of the drama, or Burns a theory of the true genesis and composition of an immortal lyric.

But while morality is possible, and this, too, of a high degree of excellence, without a definite theory of morals, it may be doubted whether any man was ever worse for trying to develop such a theory, however poorly he succeeded, so that his aim was simply to arrive at truth. If a man seeks a theory of morals that will afford an intellectual basis to a sensual or a selfish life, this is another matter. And while it is quite possible for a man to live nobly and grandly without any definite theory of morality, there are theories abroad which cannot be vitally appropriated without damage to the individual appropriating them. The man who strives persistently to educate his moral judgment, and who steadily endeavors to obey his moral impulses, can hardly miss the attainment of a lofty moral character; he cannot help going on and on to ever higher places. But even this man may be retarded in his motion by an atmosphere of thought or sentiment which he unconsciously inhales and against which he should be on his guard. Moreover, thought, the intellect, has its own rights, which ask for no ulterior sanction. Knowledge is an absolute good. Comte did not believe this, and would have had men abjure the study of sidereal astronomy because such study was not apparently useful. Enough for us that its revelations thrill us through and through with awe and adoration. So with the moral nature. We should want to fathom it, if the attempt left our moral vision exactly where it found it, clearing it no whit, nor adding one iota to the vigor of our wills. But the result is likely to be much more ample when the attempt is an unbiassed search for truth.

The subject of our discussion presents a great variety of phases, but the most important will, if I mistake not, fall under one or two general heads; namely, the origin and ground of moral distinctions, and the relation of our theoretic apprehensions of such origin and ground to the individual and social morality of the present time.

First, then, let us consider the origin and ground of moral distinctions. "Duty!" exclaims Immanuel Kant, "wondrous thought that workest neither by fond insinuation, flattery, nor any threat, but merely by upholding thy naked law to the soul, and so extorting for thyself always reverence, if not always obedience,—before whom all appetites are dumb, however secretly they rebel,—whence thy original?" Jonathan Dymond, a Quaker linen-draper, wrote a book in his back-shop, improving the intervals between his infrequent customers, which book, "Essays on the Principles of Morality," gives an unhesitating answer to Kant's passionate question, an answer mainly notable because it coincides with a very common opinion. Incidentally the book contains a great deal of excellent teaching; but I shall never forget the shock of disgust with which my mind revolted from its fundamental proposition, which is that the origin of moral distinctions is the will of God. God willed that some things should be right and others wrong, and *therefore* some things *are* right and others wrong. Here is a proposition in comparison with which John Stuart Mill's idea, that on some other planet two and two may possibly make five, seems truly admirable. If God had willed that murder, theft, adultery, and so on, should be right, they would have been. If he had willed that honesty, life-saving, chastity, and so on, should be wrong, they would have been forever. Did ever the assurance that *might makes right* receive a more significant illustration? But, as I have said, this conception of the Quaker moralist is far from being his peculiar property. It finds thousands of admirers. And it is not an isolated conception. It is of a piece with a great multitude of conceptions which regard the laws and properties of matter as having been arbitrarily imposed by the Almighty. Thus God imposed on minerals their hardness, on water or gases their mobility, on lead its malleable quality, on mercury its exceeding instability. The word "law" has been the occasion of so much mischief in these matters that it is no wonder some scientific men have wished it might be banished forever from the realm of science. This word has been interpreted by analogy with the laws which kings and parliaments impose upon their subjects. Just as these kings and parliaments impose laws upon their people, the Almighty is supposed to have imposed laws upon matter. But the truth is that there is no analogy between the laws of nature and the laws of kings and states. The laws of matter are resident in its fundamental properties; and its properties *are* fundamental. It is simply impossible to conceive of matter without properties or of nature without laws. It is sheer nonsense to talk about God's imposing properties on matter, and laws upon nature. Matter without properties and nature without laws are figments of the metaphysical and theological brain.

Now, as I have said, the notion that moral distinctions originate in the will of God is of a piece with these conceptions of natural properties and natural laws. It is a notion of sheer arbitrariness. It makes the distinction between right and wrong a purely arbitrary distinction. The distinction may still be regarded as eternal by supposing it to have been "decreed from all eternity," but if "the eternal difference between right and wrong" of which we hear so much means nothing more than this, it might date from yesterday as well. What we want is that the distinction should be genuine, that it should be real, that it should inhere in the natural relationships of actions, that it should be no veneer or varnish, but in the grain of things. Convince me that the distinction between good and evil actions is a purely arbitrary distinction, and fear of God may lead me to prefer the good and shun the evil; but there would be as little virtue in the former course as in the latter.

There have not, at any time, been wanting those who have clearly perceived the arbitrary nature of morality which has no other basis than the will of God, and these have endeavored to relieve it of its arbitrary character by imputing to the Almighty an ulterior motive. Our present life, they say, is a probation for another and a higher state of existence. The day of judgment is a competitive examination for admission to this higher state. We are fitting all our lives long for this examination. Morality is the curriculum arranged with reference to our probationary condition. The distinctions of right and wrong and the difference in actions have been created in order to furnish this curriculum. But by this subterfuge the arbitrary character of moral distinctions is in no wise affected. They remain as arbitrary as ever. They are still imposed; not necessary and essential. There is no more divinity in the atoms than there was before. In fact, to the first arbitrary distinction is now added a second. The relation of this probationary condition to a future state is purely arbitrary. No reason is given why the probation for a life of infinite duration should be limited to an average of some five and thirty years. All the reasons are opposed to any such arrangement. All the reasons are in favor of some natural and genetic relation between the life which now is and that which is to come. In short, we have here no rational account of moral distinctions.

It is the old, old story of the earth, the elephant, the tortoises. We want to know what the four tortoises are resting on; why actions are distinguished as good or bad; why some things are right and others wrong.

The transcendental moralist holds a position antipodal to that which I have been exhibiting. He contends that there is actually as well as formally an eternal difference between right and wrong. These are not mere names to him; they are things. God does not make certain actions right and others wrong by his divine decree. Rightness and wrongness inhere in actions, — in their most secret essence. Some things are right and other things are wrong in themselves. The first breath of this transcendental air is very inspiring if one enters it from the side of those arbitrary distinctions, which are not really differences, which we have been considering. But after a little while it proves as much too thin as that was too thick and heavy. We have escaped from mere arbitrariness into mere logomachy. To assert that the moral difference in actions is an essential difference, a difference in themselves, is to assert nothing. It is to fool ourselves with words. To call this difference an eternal difference is high-sounding and imposing, but it is absurd. There were no actions in the original fire-mist out of which all things have been evolved. Actions imply men. There must be men before there can be actions. But suppose — a reasonable supposition — there have been men here on the earth five hundred thousand years. This is a practical eternity. If certain actions have differed all this time as right and wrong, is it not allowable to say that the difference between them is an eternal difference? It might be if they had differed so. But they have not. Actions that are not right in one age or condition of society are right in another. The moral difference of actions is not a difference which can be estimated apart from the social order for the time being. Plants and animals can be assigned to this class or that, according as they have certain definite characteristics.

But it is not so with moral actions. Actions as nearly similar as may be are sometimes right and sometimes wrong.

And, mind you, what I mean is not that they are subjectively so. This is, no doubt, a truth, but it is a truth which has been tremendously over-emphasized, and the result has been that the objective rightness and wrongness have been overlooked. The inward disposition is much, but it is not every thing. And the presumption that it is every thing has been the fruitful mother of innumerable ills. It has prevented men's considering the consequences of their actions, as well as the purity of their intentions. It has blinded men to the New Testament principle, "No man liveth to himself, and no man dieth to himself." Jesus said that "Whosoever looketh on a woman to lust after her hath committed adultery already in his heart." But it makes a mighty difference to the social order whether a man stops at this point, or goes on to actualize his wicked thought. It makes a mighty difference to him. And this difference is one which cannot be too much insisted on. It is not enough that a man should do what he thinks is right. He must do what *is* right. For the wrong action ignorantly done brings in its train hardly less ruin of the social order than the most wilful sin. George Eliot has done no better service than in her showing of the remorseless penalties that wait on the good-natured weakness and mistaken virtue of mankind. "Danton, no weakness," said that giant of the revolution, as he drew near the guillotine. "No weakness!" That will be every man's motto who is persuaded that the motives do not trammel up the consequences of the act, and that the objective force of actions can in no wise be measured by their subjective criminality.

But this is episodical. It was suggested by the assertion that actions as nearly similar as possible are sometimes right and sometimes wrong. Why are they so over and above all reference to their subjective character? Because *the greatest good of the greatest number of actual or prospective individuals in the community, at any given time, is the end of all morality,* and this end requires at certain stages in the evolution of society a line of action which at certain other stages would be prejudicial. It does this because human nature and its environment are not constants but variable quantities, and consequently that relative harmony between the two which is essential to the best condition of society is secured by different actions at different stages of development.

This, then, is the ground of moral difference. The most useful action, this is the most right; the most useless or anti-useful, this is the most wrong. That the greatest good of the greatest number possible is the *summum bonum*, the highest possible good of society considered as a whole, would be a self-evident proposition if any thing could be. The highest possible good of any individual is certainly his greatest good. So then of every individual, and therefore of society at large. There are those who seem to think "the greatest good of the greatest number" a selfish proposition. Why not, they say, the greatest good of all? But here the part is greater than the whole. The greatest number includes all if possible. If the greatest good is not possible for all, then, evidently, the greatest good of the greatest number is the next best thing.

Such being the highest good — the fullest life, the most and purest pleasure and the least possible pain for the greatest number possible — and every action being right or wrong just in proportion as it contributes towards this highest good, how do we come to the conclusion that it is the *duty* of the individual to seek this highest good? To ask this question is to pass from the objective to the subjective side of our great theme. Duty and Ought are the great words of morality. They have exactly the same meaning. Duty is that which is due. The *ought* is that which is owed. Indeed the word "ought" is but an obsolete form of the word "owed." In Tyndale's version of the Gospels we read, "There was a certain lender which *ought* him five hundred pence." Now, if the true morality were simply the seeking of one's private happiness, as some Utilitarians have contended, I do not see that there would be any place in such morality for these great words. When George Eliot says of Captain Wybrow that he "did what was pleasant and agreeable to him from a sense of duty," she writes one of the most biting sarcasms ever written. So long as a man is doing merely what is pleasant and agreeable to him, and making this the end of his morality, the sense of duty has no fellowship with him. When we speak of a man's owing such and such things to himself, we are generally excusing his selfishness, or justifying his extravagance, or implying that he owes something to other people. The words "ought" and "duty" have no place in the scheme of *individual hedonism*, the pursuit of individual happiness as the highest good. Their only rightful place is in that *universal hedonism* which seeks the greatest good of the greatest number. But why ought the individual to seek the greatest good of all? Because it is self-evident that every other individual has an equal right with him to the highest possible good. But right and duty are but different sides of one stupendous fact. Every man's right is all men's duty; and, conversely, all men's right is every individual's duty. The right of all men to the greatest possible good, the fullest possible life, demonstrates the duty of each individual to seek the highest good of all.

And is this the Utilitarianism which is so often spoken of in terms of pity and contempt? No, this is the Utilitarianism which is so misconceived that men speak of their misconception in such terms, as well they may. If the only Utilitarianism were that which prizes all things at their money value, then, indeed, it might well merit all the scorn that men could heap upon it. Or if the only Utilitarianism were that which leads the individual to seek his individual happiness, then would the word "Utilitarianism" be one of the largest words for one of the smallest things under the cope of heaven. But because Utilitarianism, as conceived by all its best expositors, is that system of morality which makes the greatest good of the greatest number the necessary goal of individual effort, those who call themselves Utilitarians have no need to apologize for their creed. Rather they ought to hesitate before they dare count themselves worthy to be marshalled under such a flag. There is no taint of selfishness or sordidness in such a creed. There is no possible splendor of self-sacrifice which cannot find full room to exercise itself within its ample scope.

Compare the Utilitarian ground of moral distinctions, as thus conceived, with that of Jonathan Dymond and his school, — the will of God. It may not sound so fine to ears attuned to theological phrases and to these alone, but it differs from it as reality differs from a hollow show. One says that *might makes right*, the other that *use makes right*, the highest use, the fullest possible life of the greatest number of mankind. Compare this Utilitarian ground of moral distinctions with the high-sounding transcendental dictum, We should do right because it is right. There is a meaning of these words which God forbid we should not honor with our deepest admiration, a meaning which every true man can cordially agree to, for it is that we are not to do right from ulterior, selfish motives. We are not to do right through any hope of heaven, or any fear of hell, — through any zeal sectarian or partisan, or with any view of increasing our own reputation, popularity, or wealth. But in all strictness, this expression, "We should do right because it is right," is an identical proposition; that is, it predicates nothing. The predicate is but a repetition of the subject, as if one should say, "A horse is a horse." As a formula of moral philosophy, as expressive of the ground of right action, this identical proposition is of no account. There would be no special virtue in doing a thing because it is right, if this word "right" did not have a definite meaning. The right is that which is most useful to humanity. What is the most useful, mankind has been trying to discover these half-million years, and it has got a little way, but it has a long, long way to go.

It is suggested that the transcendental dictum, "We should do right because it is right," has about it an air of mystery which is indispensable to ethical authority. But mystery, which is the outcome of mere ignorance and negation, does not appeal to rational men with any gesture of authority. The mystery which has this gesture, and a voice to match, is the mystery of an order of development so vast that we can only apprehend some little segment of it here and there; we cannot trace its infinite parabola. If in its practical working the outcome of Utilitarianism were that every individual should begin *de novo*, and elaborate for himself a scheme of uses and look up to his scheme as his authority, I grant you that there would be something petty in his attitude. There would be a lack of noble mystery pertaining to his sense of duty. It would not be natural for such a man to respond very deeply to Wordsworth's "Ode to Duty," to say to her, —

> "Thou dost preserve the stars from wrong,
> And the most ancient heavens through thee are fresh and strong."

"But," as one of your own prophets hath said, "let us take into account the great principle "of heredity; let the sense of utility, of the "needs of society, of the demands which the "whole makes upon each part, have gathered "strength through innumerable generations; let "all irregularities of time and place be elimi- "nated from the result, because such irregu- "larities will go for nothing in the great mass; "and let the combined, intensified, and puri- "fied result enter into the constitution of the "individual; let it be born with him, and "twined with every fibre of his brain," and we should then have "the elements of a "mysterious authority, whose decisions are not "to be questioned or explained, which acts "from the depth of nature, and which thus "represents the categorical imperative that we "seek."[1]

And if, in its latest stages, Utilitarian morality does not imply that every moral act is based upon an individual calculation of the relation of such an act to the greatest good of the greatest number, still less does it imply this in its earliest stages. No wonder that Utilitarianism seems absurd when it is conceived as picturing the primeval savage debating with himself whether the act to which he is impelled has in it the quality of universal usefulness. No wonder that it still seems absurd when our present moral intuitions are regarded as the outcome of innumerable conscious generalizations in the past, transmitted to us along the lines of our hereditary qualities. But these are men of straw, set up by stealth with a view to being demolished with great public distinction. The true Utilitarian does not imagine

[1] The New Ethics, by Professor C. C. Everett, of the Divinity School, Harvard University; — an exceedingly suggestive and comprehensive article in the Unitarian Review, October, 1878.

that the primeval savage consciously presented to himself either the idea of general or individual use. Given that "stream of tendency in virtue of which every thing tends to fulfil the law of its being,"—given this stream, not in an isolated individual, but in a multitude of individuals living together and forming a society,—and immediately the desires begin to clash. Two men want the same thing. They cannot both have it. On every side man finds his impulses checked and thwarted by his fellow-man. So long as men attempt to act out these impulses freely, without regard to each other, life is intolerable, full of violence and robbery and domestic anarchy. Instead of fulfilling the law of their being, men find that they are standing in each other's way; that, so long as it is every man for himself, the devil takes, not merely the hindmost, but almost everybody. And hence arises the perception — a perception instinctive and unconscious — that, in a world where much is wanted, much must be resigned; that men need each other; that there is a "law of liberty." This law of liberty is the moral law, the perception of which, with the corresponding sense that it must be obeyed, is conscience, — *con-science*, that which men know together. How many confluents, from first to last, flow into this before the tiny stream becomes a mighty river, fertilizing history for ages down with its unfailing flood! Darwin's gregariousness is no doubt its fountain-head. If man were not a social animal, if he could live apart from all his kind, the stress of circumstances would not develop the law of liberty and the corresponding moral sense. It is only when men live together, and begin to suffer inconvenience from the free and unrestrained exercise of each other's wills, that the sense of mutual obligation is developed.

What more natural than that sympathy, *sun-pathos*, common feeling, should be immensely productive of conscience, *con-science*, common knowledge, men's knowledge of the principles which ought to regulate their common life? Sympathy, the power of ideally presenting to one's self the feelings of another person, was never better indicated than in that pathetic sentence of Eugénie de Guérin, "I feel a pain in my brother's side." Many such pains went to the shaping of the moral sense of the primeval man. In his dealings with others he found himself avoiding those things which gave him pain, doing the things which would allay its smart, praising those persons who avoided hurtful things, and blaming those who did not avoid them, and so on. Thus praise and blame began to play their part, a mighty one it has since proved, in strengthening in men's minds the sense of mutual obligation.

Well said the Psalmist, "Out of the mouths of babes and sucklings hast thou ordained praise," for to the feebleness of human infancy more than to any other cause are we apparently indebted for the placing of "the solitary in families," the strengthening of domestic ties. If it had been possible to "cast the bantling on the rocks," the genesis of the family would seemingly have been impossible. But, as it was, those tiny hands, "with love's invisible sceptre laden," held father and mother together till, through force of habit, they became necessary to each other's happiness, and permanent family relations were thus engendered. So out of the physical weakness and consequent prolongation of human infancy, as distinguished from that of other primates, was perfected the moral strength of "the first families" of primitive civilization, developing in time into that of the clan and tribe, and then, with ever-widening sympathy, at last into "the enthusiasm for humanity."

Do not imagine that in this process of evolution from mere gregariousness to universal philanthropy there has been no admixture of unreal and superstitious elements. The sentiment of Duty, of the Ought, — that which is owed, — has received immense accession from the apotheosis of the chief and king, henceforth conceived as the legislator and executor of those moral laws which are the expressions of the average sense of the community as to what lines of conduct are most conducive to the general good. If this were the whole story, how different the history of humanity would have been! But, alas! the imaginary gods have also been conceived as claiming for themselves hundreds of duties over and above the claims of men upon each other. To this day men conceive that they have innumerable duties to God which are in no sense duties which they owe each other. Indeed, now, as always, the imaginary duty to God is often in direct conflict with the obvious duty to mankind. If all the strength which, from the beginning, has gone to men's imaginary duties to God, could have gone to their obvious and acknowledged duties to each other, how different would be the aspect of our race to-day!

Professor Everett says, "If the new morality "would in any sense replace the old, it must be "shown to have at least the authority of an "instinct." Such an authority is claimed for it by its most competent expositors, and I have given you an inkling of the method of their proof. It disposes for ever of the imaginary Utilitarian, debating, on the threshold of each separate action, its probable effect upon the greatest good of the greatest number. It disposes for ever of the conception of Utilitarian morality as the hereditary sum-total of the reasoned results of by-gone generations in regard to what constitutes the greatest good of the greatest number. But what is true is, that our modern conscience is the product of innumerable instinctive efforts of past generations to adjust the units of society in such relative positions as should give rise to the least possible friction, the utmost fulness of life. "The experiences of utility organized and consolidated through all past generations of the human race have been producing corresponding modifications, which by transmission and accumulation have become in us certain faculties of moral intuition."[1]

So much for the origin and ground of the distinctions between right and wrong. These

---

[1] Herbert Spencer.

distinctions are not merely nominal. They are real; they are inseparable from the social life of man. Given men living in society, and there must be such distinctions. Nor are we put off any longer with identical propositions. To do right because it is right, has still a glorious meaning, but it gives no reason why we *should* do right, nor any intimation in what the right consists. The ethics of evolution do give such a reason, — do furnish such an intimation. The intimation is, that right is the science necessary to *the art of living together;* the reason is, that, as all owe us the practice of this art, so we owe it to all.

And now, very briefly, let us consider the relation of this theory of morals to the individual and social morality of the present time. Where shall men go to find the separate precepts of this Utilitarian morality? The happy people who believe that moral distinctions originate in the will of God generally believe, at the same time, that the Bible is a revelation of the will of God. Here is their moral code. Here, but where? In the Old Testament or the New? In the Proverbs or the Psalms? In the Gospels or Epistles? Where the injunctions are easiest, or where they are the hardest? As a rule, where they are easiest. Men never tire of talking very sweetly about the Sermon on the Mount. They never think of realizing its injunctions in their personal concerns. But even if we believed the will of God to be the source of moral distinctions, we could not accept the Bible as a revelation of his will. We do not know who wrote the most of it, or when it was written, and the writers seldom claim, and never show, a supernatural inspiration. Where then shall the Utilitarian moralist go to find the separate precepts of the code he is to follow? To Herbert Spencer or John Stuart Mill? They have not deigned to furnish us with such a code. And there was little need for them to do so. The word is very near us, even in our hearts. The experience of the ages is organized in us. And it is also organized in other men and women everywhere about us, in some much more perfectly than in others, and in hundreds of great poems and noble books. Therefore it is that in the great majority of cases we have no doubt whatever what we ought to do. If we should stop to analyze the moral laws which, at every turn, claim our obedience, we should find that every one of them is a rough expression of Utilitarian considerations. But these laws appeal to us, not as useful, but as right. Only when the element of doubt comes in, and any law that claims obedience has to be tested, do we perceive that utility is the basis of right, the widest possible utility. All do not pursue this method. Some appeal to the Bible, — now for some righteous cause, and anon for an excuse to take a little wine for their stomach's sake, or to gag a woman with a text, or to send back a fugitive slave; and all do not apply the standard of the widest possible utility. They would have their party or their country flourish at the expense of those beyond; and so they institute protective tariffs and prohibit foreign immigration. This is the morality of the clan.

Jesus said, "Unless your righteousness exceed that of the Scribes and Pharisees, you shall in no wise enter into the kingdom of God." And yet the Scribes and Pharisees were the most righteous people of his time. There is a suggestion here, that a much higher morality is still possible for mankind than that demanded by our present intuitions. The inter-adjustments of society are still far enough from being perfect. But the more perfect adjustment will not come from the side of rampant individualism. The passion for freedom has done a great and glorious work, and it has still much to do. But there is less hope for humanity in this passion than in the willingness to be greatly bound, — the willingness to subordinate individual comfort and desire to an extended common good.

Because the measure of morality is the greatest good of the greatest number, there are those who seem to think that a Utilitarian must try to spread himself in the thinnest possible layer over the surface of humanity, or that he must neglect his morning errands for the claims of Borroboolagha. But no: the best expositors of our creed assure us that we can best assist the good of all by doing our most obvious duty in the sphere of our immediate relationships of love and labor.

A great deal is said of sanctions of morality, a great deal more than would be if men were deeply impressed with the Utilitarian idea. This seeking for sanctions,—what is it for the most part but an unconscious confession that the law of right contains no reason in itself why it should be obeyed? To the trained Utilitarian it is a sufficient sanction of morality that it is the bond of social order, the means of realizing the fullest possible life of the community. Of those who have much to say about moral sanctions, that is, reasons why we should obey the moral law, many are continually assuring us that morality acquires all its value and sacredness from the idea of immortality, the relation of this life to another. Take away immortality, they say, and there is no reason why a man should try to do his duty; and yet the very men who talk in this manner accuse Utilitarian morality of selfishness. Was ever a more flagrant instance of the pot calling the kettle black? Only the kettle in this instance is an imaginary kettle. The real one is not black. The real Utilitarian, the *universal hedonist*, is not selfish in his theory of life. To live for all is surely not the creed of selfishness. But what shall we say to this idea that without immortality there is no reason why a man should do his duty? This: that such an idea is a degradation of both immortality and morality. This also: that the idea is absurd. If I were a day-fly I would get as much as possible into my day. Though we should have our be-all and our end-all here, morality would still be the means of assuring the greatest good of the greatest number. I have heard of a child who had an apple in each hand, to whom a third was offered. Whereupon, unable to grasp it, he threw down the two he had, and burst into a flood of tears. Was it a true story, or only a witty parable of the popular religionist, who, with his hands full of benefits, throws them away, and bursts into a baby's cry because he cannot grasp the fruit of immortality?

"Is there no second life? 'Pitch this one high." Is this a familiar quotation? It cannot be too familiar. A man does not deserve the hope of immortality who cannot put it to a better use than this of a mere bribe to human selfishness; and what is more, when morality is so degraded, the noblest argument for immortality is gone. For what is this but the inconceivability of the extinction of an unselfish soul? But the extinction of such worms and flies as men would be who could not keep the moral law but for the prize of immortality, is by no means inconceivable.

Again, it is insisted that without a dogmatic belief in a personal God morality is impossible. But Benedict Spinoza, the God of whose belief was certainly not personal, in any ordinary meaning of the word, had such a genius for morality as few other men have had in all the history of thought. I yield to no man in the depth and joy of my assurance of an Infinite Life which men call God, as good a name as any for the Unnamable. But I rejoice to see that the moral law is so deeply implicated in the structure of society that it does not depend for its authority or sanction upon any theory of the Infinite, or even upon any conscious theistic affirmation.

> "Sits there no judge in heaven our sin to see?
> More strictly then the inward judge obey."

Here is this world, — this human world, — and, God or no God, morality is the art of life, the necessary condition of the greatest good of the greatest number. Is it, as pessimism thinks, the worst possible world? If so, without a God, then let us make the best of it we can, and better it a little for the men and women who will live when we are dead and gone. If with a God, then, in all reverence, as Hartmann thinks, we must pity him, poor God! and do our best to take a little from his pain.

"Forgive these wild and wandering cries."

They do but hide under their seeming blasphemy the strength of our inalienable conviction that morality is too deeply implicated in the life of man to be at the mercy of any theory or no-theory of God or the immortal life. Whenever two or three or more are gathered together, there is the Holy Spirit, conscience, in the midst of them.

And is there, then, no point of contact between morality and worship, the sense of duty and the sense of God? I have not said this, and I do not believe it. I believe with Matthew Arnold, that there is a power, not ourselves, that makes for righteousness. And by "ourselves" I do not mean just our immediate selves. I mean all men and women that ever lived. I believe there is an eternal power not ourselves that makes for righteousness, eternal in no metaphorical sense, but absolutely eternal. I believe that this power not ourselves is the Infinite Being, God. I believe that Wordsworth wrote, not merely poetry, but truth when he wrote, as I have quoted once already, apostrophizing duty, —

"Thou dost preserve the stars from wrong,
 And the most ancient heavens through thee are fresh and strong."

Why, but because it is the same infinite power "whose pulses wave-like beat on shore of sun and star and still flow on from heaven to heaven everlastingly," whose genius is more grandly evident in the out-goings of the moral life of man? There is no break in the long line of evolution.

"The world was once a fluid haze of light,
 Till toward the centre set the starry tides
 And eddied into suns, that wheeling cast
 The planets; then the monster; then the man."

And man discovered in himself an impulse to morality. He discovered it. He did not invent it.

"God kindly gave his blood a moral flow."

And so morality becomes religious. Without consciously affirming God, a man may still be moral. But without the God whom some cannot affirm, there could be no morality, no man, no universe.

Men have conceived themselves as having duties to God which are in no wise duties to man. But the new ethics recognize no such duties. The catalogue is exhausted by our duties to each other and our poor relations, the dumb animals as we call them, because we do not understand their speech any better than they do ours. I sometimes wonder if they think us also dumb. But though our Utilitarian morality recognizes no separate duty to God, it recognizes joyfully that all our duties to each other are equally duties to him, his dues, that which we owe to him. For see, the All is for each one of us. And what is the inevitable response of any earnest heart that knows and feels the truth of this,—that all is so for each, that One, the Infinite, is so for all? What can it be but, Each for all, Each for the Infinite One. So grandly helped, we long to help in turn. But how? We cannot make the sun any brighter, or the sky any bluer, or the ocean or the mountains any more sublime. Here and there we can make the earth a little greener, fairer; perhaps make such a flower to bloom as God has never seen before in all the eternal years. But this is not enough. We must do more than this; and the way is always clear; the gate is always open. It is *to lend a hand,*— to do what in us lies to make life happier, sweeter, cleaner, brighter, holier, diviner, for those with whom we mingle in the various activities of life and love, and those who will succeed to our inheritance of beauty, truth, and good. Thus worship at its best becomes morality, while, at the same time, morality becomes religion, all duties to our fellow-men becoming duties to Him who,

> 'be he what he may,
> Is yet the fountain light of all our day,
> Is yet the master light of all our seeing.'

And this is "mere morality." Oh, long despised, the day is drawing nigh when men shall see that thou art the most beautiful and strong and grandly dowered of all the masters of the world! Thou art the builder and preserver of all families and states. Thou art the joy and confidence of all the earth. There is no happiness like thine, albeit it is "a sort of "happiness which often brings so much pain with "it that we can only tell it from pain by its "being that which we would choose before every "thing else, because our souls see it to be good."

> Thou whose name is blazoned forth
> On our banner's gleaming fold,
> Freedom! thou whose sacred worth
> Never yet has half been told!
> Often have we sung of thee,
> Dear to us as dear can be.
>
> But to-day we sing of one
> Older, graver far than thou;
> With the seal of time begun
> Stamped upon her awful brow.
> Freedom, latest born of time,
> Knowest thou her form sublime?
>
> She is Duty; in her hand
> Is a sceptre, heaven-wrought;
> Hers the accent of command;
> Hers the dreadful, mystic Ought;
> Hers upon us all to lay
> Heavier burdens every day.

But her bondage is so sweet!
   And her burdens make us strong;
Wings they seem to weary feet,
   Laughter to our lips and song.
Freedom, make us free to speed
Wheresoever she may lead!

FEBRUARY 23, 1879.

www.ingramcontent.com/pod-product-compliance
Lightning Source LLC
Chambersburg PA
CBHW020758230426
43666CB00007B/754